# Awakening Wisdom from Innocence

### By

### Dolores Calley

© 2002 by Dolores Calley. All rights reserved.

No part of this book may be reproduced, stored in a retrieval system, or transmitted by any means, electronic, mechanical, photocopying, recording, or otherwise, without written permission from the author.

ISBN: 1-4033-1813-1 (e-book)
ISBN: 1-4033-1814-X (Paperback)

Library of Congress Control Number: 2002105703

This book is printed on acid free paper.

Printed in the United States of America
Bloomington, IN

1stBooks - rev. 07/13/02

*To my Mother*
*Who walked with me*
*Through the forest*
*And*
*To my children*
*Who gave me reason*
*To look anew as*
*I walked with them*

# Acknowledgements

Any literary work carries within its words the input and support of those who are part of the authors circle of friends. Knowing this truth I am deeply grateful to those who have contributed to this book. The group consists of my family and dear friends. I wish to thank those who have read and commented on my writing, my cousin Cathie and her daughter Shannon, my brother Rick, my Mother, my friends Renate and Judy. My friend Anthony, an older single man, also belongs in the list for he helped me realize that, since we are all former children, those struggling with childhood issues may find peace and understanding from the book. Roy, a former high school English teacher, was a splendid editor. He patiently taught me high school grammar as well as build my confidence as an author through his commentary and ability to make connections between my work and that of other published authors. The creative team consists of my sister Cathy the artist who generously provided the cover picture. Heidi was also invaluable with her creativity and computer skills.

*Only love endures*

# Introduction

Since childhood I have believed in a society based on unconditional love and support. When I was little I used to gaze at the stars and wait for someone to come and take home. At present, this has not happened. I am still here.

Still a believer, but having grown more mature in the ways of the world and having developed an awareness of my own personal power, I have come to the conclusion that perhaps I, and all of the other optimists who make up modern, western society are suppose to create this loving, supportive community. Even though many human beings may torment themselves and each other, toss major obstacles on their individual paths, perceive many more flaws and weaknesses than talents and achievements, the species of Homo Sapiens is abundantly gifted. One needs only reflect upon the accomplishments of the average baby in the first two years of life. Within that time frame a child has established a place in the world. With no inkling of where he or she has landed, the child teaches himself or herself to communicate, walk, eat, interact with other people, express gratitude, find answers, and a multitude of other necessary skills required to function well in society. Beyond the necessities, the child dreams, imagines, and delights in the world around him or her.

Almost everyone enjoys babies and little children. All too often I hear adults say that children are wonderful until they grow to be six or seven years old. Then adults often seems to prefer hiding children away someplace until they grow into adults.

The change in opinion of children coincides with their becoming students in the public school system. Something happens during this period when the child moves into a focus of individual awareness and the establishment of ego. Within many families the child spends less time with family, growing under the watchful, all seeing, guiding eyes of the teacher and other caregivers. The molding of personality continues as the child strives to reestablish himself or herself in a group of many other children learning discipline, setting aside intuitive guidance for authoritarian direction, and submitting to comparative evaluation. Punishment may first be encountered at school and fear of punishment is reinforced regularly. Fear, judgment, and expectations become the silent directors of development.

The major change in the view of children as they mature suggest that something should be done to preserve the childhood attributes that so delight and invigorate society while still supporting the process of human development and maturation within a cultural framework. Maybe adults suffer from an overabundance of struggle, neurosis, isolation, and inner turmoil because of the path alteration that began in their fifth or sixth year of life. My heart knows that there are some aspects of socializtion, which formally begins with schooling, that need reevaluation. Some desired cultural behaviors conflict with the very nature of the human spirit. As the inner turmoil builds, behavior modification methods become more severe, forcing the spirit to work harder to reestablish balance with the essence of the individual. The time is ripe for a change based on an awareness of what it means to be human. A conscious choice can be made to support and work with the nature of being human and to design a culture that builds upon the beauty of the new, innocent being. There is a great wisdom in that innocence.

If there are other people who yearn for a kinder, more cooperative, and accepting society, we need to join together, understand the present situation, determine what can and should be changed, explore creative options to support children in successful development, begin the process of eliminating that which is not working, and establish a new framework for a refreshed society. Human beings have an immense untapped potential waiting to contribute creative ideas for the establishment of a loving, supportive, cooperative unity of unique individuals. The reality of such a society is a matter of choice, one individual at a time. Indigenous peoples have many models of predominately harmonious, peaceful communities that could serve as templates. The simple beliefs of tribal societies could be intertwined with the conveniences and wonders of technology, truly acknowledgeing and accepting the diversity of the peoples of the earth.

A new millennium heralds the reflection of advancing age and the innocent hope of youth to bring forth a better world. The stage is set for the forgotten wisdom of the innocent to clasp hands with the wisdom of experience.

Proceed, please, with an open mind and a thinking brain. Forget about challenging or embracing my thoughts and observations. Rather use my ideas as stepping-stones into your own authentic ideas and beliefs. Allow yourself to marvel at the beautifully designed, interwoven pattern of your own set of life experiences. Delight yourself with the precision of your thinking brain as it begins to make the connections that have been waiting a lifetime for your recognition.

Look at where you have come from and where you are leading your children. Daydream abut a community that has been created with components you deem important. Then decide with your own freedom of choice how you can participate in bringing forth the ideal culture.

# Contents

I. Priorities, Vulnerability, and Trust ........................................ 1

II. Play, Focus, and Creativity .................................................. 32

III. Potential, Intuition, and Adaptation ..................................... 57

IV. Expectations, Judgment, and Fear...................................... 84

V. Diversity, Unity, and Acceptance ...................................... 111

VI. Communication, Gratitude, and Love............................... 135

VII. Truth, Personal Power, and Responsibility....................... 158

VIII. Honor, Courage, and Respect ............................................ 180

IX. Forgiveness, Compassion, and Freedom........................... 200

# Chapter 1

# Priorities, Vulnerability, and Trust

"For the children" is a mantra voiced again and again in addressing priorities on both a federal and family level. In the area of governmental issues, environmentalists, economists, accountants, and the like often ask Americans to consider future generations when prioritizing programs. In theory this consideration is healthy and appropriate, but it is often used as the emotional hook to draw the support of individuals for a moneymaking agenda. In those cases the children are being used for someone's personal gain.

On the home front, mothers and fathers decide to take on additional employment to provide a better life for their families. This is often done for the children. Sometimes parent work schedules leave young children in the care of others for daytime hours or home alone with the companionship of television and video game characters. Parental devotion to maintaining and fulfilling job responsibilities often leaves parents with little time or energy left over to enjoy their growing youngsters. At best, enjoyable family time occurs a few times throughout the year on holidays and vacation.

Going a step further, the amount of single parent households due to divorce and unplanned pregnancy is high. This situation makes it next to impossible to satisfy the financial demands of a comfortable home and still have time to come together as a loving, supportive family. A single parent is often absent from the home front because of need and desperation. I know; I have been there.

All of these circumstances base part of their development on the needs of the children. In the list of priorities, the adults, who have greater control, assess the child's need for parental love, companionship, attention, and support near the bottom of the list. Much higher on the list are things like a college fund, a popular video system, dancing lessons, math tutor, summer camp, big screen TV, minivan, Ritalin, preschool, and other items and services. Somehow in the cry "for the children", society has forgotten the children. They, like the aging members of society, are looked upon as a group of problems to be addressed expediently so the work of the nation can move full speed ahead.

Both the old and the young are isolated in peer groups, sustained, and entertained so that the work force can operate efficiently, focusing on the goal of the nation. That consensus objective of production and consumerism feeds on the labor of many, leaving most families to exist on the crumbs left after the lion has eaten. In the process many children in today's society develop in an atmosphere of isolation, lacking a secure source of love, a continuous stable supply of encouragement and validation, and safe opportunities to explore the world and their own talents.

In light of this bizarre childhood, is it any wonder that school violence, drug and alcohol abuse, teen pregnancy, and teen suicide continue to confound and confront society? I find it much more amazing that any child, neglected, battered, and forgotten by such a wealthy and powerful country, grows up well. The process of growing into adulthood and finding a satisfying and sustainable place in society does not have to be so hard.

Looking at the adult segment of society, one again often sees a continuation of isolation, abuse, and despair, only now there is also a heavy yoke of responsibility and a powerful whip of rules. No matter how clean the air becomes, how often one proves their expertise through testing, or how legally accountable a company is for their product's performance, the well being of the people holds the key to enjoying life and evolving into a satisfying, supportive community for all.

The children are the ones who know the mystery behind the locked door. Since each person has started as a child, everyone knew the mystery. The children serve to remind society of the innocent wisdom of just being. They stand as spiritual teachers of the peaceful simplicity of being human. For their service and gift to humanity, children should be honored, respected, and assured a safe haven in which to grow. They must become a top priority!

Ask any parent of a dying, or better yet my personal favorite, a suicidal child, if they would give up their home, their money, their job, and their credit cards to restore the health of their child. In this type of circumstance, suddenly, the career that has taken years and money to establish seems almost a waste, because relative to the loss of a child the career has little meaning. After all it's easy to build another career; the child is irreplaceable. Something this dramatic, this significant, brings one humbly back to the source of what is truly meaningful in life, and it does so quickly and vividly.

There are almost always signs that are often lost in the business of life. If the gentle messages have not sounded a wake up call, the parents will not ignore one that directly puts their child in jeopardy. On a grander scale, the displays of hostility and despair that society is witnessing from children today indicate something is painfully wrong. As the decision making body of society, adults need to face their responsibility and address childhood issues.

Grave experiences, where the child is on the line, points up how our societal focus encourages individuals to spend lots of time collecting items that are not needed for their well-being and minimizing the importance of the people and things their life and well-being depends upon. Take a moment and find the last hour of play you have had with your child, the last conversation about life beliefs and purpose, or the last "I love you" hug given with real emotion. If you are going back weeks or months, maybe you are missing some very relevant and rewarding experiences that your family is waiting to share with you. It's okay to rationalize the long hours at work or the second job's income as time spent supporting your children, but is that what they really need or what they would choose given the option. If your priorities need to be rearranged, and you do not choose to adjust them in your own manner, your child can and probably will help you recognize the need. Teenagers are very adept at forcing their parents to address problems that have been ignored for years. Inevitably, the realization will improve life for the family.

Trust and vulnerability lessons are part of the example of the death or illness of a child, but they are also a regular occurrence with children in the household. Most people would cheerfully break their right arm in place of their injured child so that they don't have to suffer through the cries and sorrowful look of their son or daughter. Instead, they are called upon to rise above their vulnerability and support their dear one. Generally, the parents accomplish this successfully by trusting that the doctor knows what she is doing, that the body has remarkable healing powers, and that time will ease the pain. Even with that knowledge, I have always been grateful to see my children safely grow through another year.

*Awakening Wisdom from Innocence*

When my son was about seven or eight, he desperately wanted the freedom of riding his bike in the neighborhood. It made him feel cool, free, and independent. Me, I was petrified he'd get hit by a car. Absolutely anything I could punish him for, I did. I just took away his bike, and I felt a lot better, too. He, of course, suffered major frustration.

This action on my part definitely caused friction between us. At a point of utter frustration, I sat down with my son, John, and said, "I'm really worried that you will get hit by a car. That's why I'm always taking your bike away. Do you have any ideas on what we can do so I don't worry or take your bike away?"

Together we came up with some positive steps to take. John would tell me where he wanted to ride to and let me know as soon as he returned. We also agreed upon safe bike riding rules, and I watched him ride to make sure he used them. My confidence grew as I took an interest in his biking. I learned that he was very capable with his bike because I participated in his interest. As my faith grew in response to John's diligence we could both relax.

*Dolores Calley*

Even when John graduated to a 1976 Corvette, I worried a lot less than most parents. Early on John and I had established a connection that recognized my vulnerability, and I was confident that John would keep me informed and call if he needed me.

John was a very capable teacher because he saw and understood what I needed to feel secure. He allowed me to grow in acquiring the trust to depend on him to follow through with what we discussed. Together we also worked on communicating our often-conflicting needs. Through this experience I developed a greater appreciation of the reliability of young children, and John became an independent and dependable guy.

This seemingly little lesson was comfortable in that each of us took as much time as we required. This lesson spanned years, deepening and stretching, incorporating whatever flexibility was needed for many moments that followed. And this occurred because, for a time, John's bike riding became a joint priority. Time was made, John's desires were respected, and together we reinforced love and built a communication pathway.

Only the passage of time allowed me to realize there was much personal gain for me by fulfilling my role in this little drama. In a very real way, I was learning how to communicate my needs and build trust in the actions of those around me. Having suffered a few major blows to trusting people, especially myself, I used this opportunity to regain faith in people. My son harbored a safe, loving port from which to set sail. Not all that many years later, my other child would push me much deeper into the very depths of trust, allowing me to explore my faith with the unseen world as well as with those present in my life. I had reached a plateau and was prepared for a deeper lesson.

Suicide. My dear Wendel spent three years in a place I have yet to fully understand, a despair that takes over and begs for the darkness of death. Talk about opportunities that challenged my priorities, forced me to face my vulnerabilities, and encouraged blind faith, blind, because you can't see who is carrying you through the day.

Talk about priorities. I suddenly wanted to wipe the slate clean, forget about my other child, working, maintaining a household, and sit, and watch my child until the "badness" went away. But I couldn't. I simply had to find some balance, and I had to do this when my own frailty was magnifying all my insecurities and wiping out any vestiges of confidence that I had spent a lifetime gathering.

If any one identifies with such emotional upheaval, my advice is to find a friend who will bolster your confidence by allowing you to share absolutely anything without judgment, and who will help you see what you are feeling. Situations like this demand decision after decision, and if the wrong choice is made, the failure would be a major big one.

Having a friend who meets most of the qualifications, I gingerly tested the water, because there was nothing but water around me. And I am AFRAID OF WATER! Immediately, the water encircled my feet and swirled around me, engulfing my body. It pulled me under again and again. Fear often does that.

As I was walking around in this perpetual state of near drowning, my other child was begging, "I'm hungry." The bills were demanding, "Pay me." And the workplace was wordlessly throwing another task my way. How could I organize such priorities?

For me the motto was "I won't be tested beyond what I can bear." This was united with the adage, "take it one day at a time," although I did at times modify it to one hour at a time. Armed with these seemingly flimsy tenets, I faced my life and reaffirmed my own strength and power (thank you Wendel), so that I could become an anchor for Wendel in the sea of despair we now shared.

Years would pass before I could appreciate anything positive from this experience, but it would come. The lesson and the growth for both of us have been significant. As for priorities, I did give Wendel the top spot on the list. Anytime, day or night, I was available either in person or by phone. At work friends covered for me if I had to leave, and my manager was wonderful and understanding. Wendel thought nothing of calling a restaurant or store looking for me. Sometimes it was a royal pain, but if a listening ear was going to keep him from harming himself, he had it from me. I expect this situation also held the early lessons of unconditional love. Because of Wendel's anger, I was often available for verbal abuse.

A good part of this availability was for myself. I had felt guilty for as long as I could remember about the rotten life I had given my children. Can you imagine the guilt I could wallow in if I had missed a needy moment, and Wendel did himself in? There could be no second chance, and a horrible thing could happen in little more than the blink of an eye.

My heart may have been in the right place, but my body couldn't continue with such an overwhelming imbalance of priorities. For a short term, it's probably okay, but Wendel's suicide attempts spanned a period of years. Add to the active suicide attempt period, Wendel needed recovery time and an adjustment period when reentering the realm of the living. It is not easy to just flip the day on the calendar and say, "Good! Today Wendel is no longer suicidal. I'm glad that's over." Thus, an opportunity to further delve into priorities.

Life does go on even under dire conditions. Wendel had good days and bad days, but I lived, maybe we both lived, with death sitting, grinning at me as I took each breath. I am strong, but I was weakening. Aside from the fact that I had little sleep, served as Wendel's 24 hour a day therapist, worked, cooked, and dealt with life's other demands, Wendel's suicidal behavior was but a part of other self-destructive behaviors. Within weeks I had to look at myself as a priority.

Not only was I becoming a total raw nerve with baggy, blood shot eyes, but I had another child I was ignoring, a job I felt I was short changing, and a desperate need for some peaceful, personal time. If I was going to be of any benefit to anyone, Wendel included, I had to quickly address my personal issues.

In order to begin to let go of the fear I had for Wendel, I had to decide how I felt about death. Does a person cease to exist in death, and if not, what is the new reality like? If there would be an end to torment, would that be a better world for Wendel; could I live with that outcome? Inevitably, the important issue for me became working through the worst scenario and finding a way to accept and live with it. So, as I was moving through my fear of death, I guess Wendel was moving through his fear of continuing to live.

My father had died when I was ten years old. At that time my family was in such sad shape that I focused on being responsible and helping with all the little daily routines. There was little time to allow my feelings regarding the death of someone I deeply loved to become a priority. Too many other family members were already doing that. And most of the time, the atmosphere was much too torrential for any more sorrow. By the time my mother and siblings had reawakened to life, I had tucked away my grief. Little did I realize that my own child would find the door to the chamber of pain within me and wrench it open. Wendel forced me to once again explore my feelings and beliefs about the loss of a loved one. He gave me the opportunity to face the issue and resolve the residual feeling of loss from my father's death.

Now, having cleared and lighted that shrouded place, I can honestly appreciate one of the lessons Wendel's torment inspired for me. Through his despair I could begin to address a deep despair that had long ago become a part of my being. This time I would be able to face it, address the issues surrounding it, and achieve a much greater level of harmony within myself. Wendel allowed me the chance to view this aspect from an adult perspective. By putting himself on the line, my love for Wendel demanded a healing of my wound so that I would have the strength necessary to support Wendel in his despair.

Whether or not the worst scenario manifested for Wendel and me, the possibility was a powerful lesson. Through this experience, the near loss of a loved one, I became a priority to myself, and the possibility of having to continue life without my beloved child was faced and explored. Now I am here, able to share my growth. During this period I uncovered a belief in transition rather than death. Ironically, my father's presence during these difficult years was palpable. I know he was with both Wendel and me. Wendel had pushed me to seek faith in the unseen and to expand my awareness of different ways to communicate, not only with the world of spirit, but with my son who often presented as a far from rational individual.

Learning to trust in something or someone that cannot be seen, but only felt is remarkable freeing. Suddenly, there is no more worry, no desire for control, and little expectation about the final outcome. It's a support that is reliable and available when no one else is around. It's a friendship that doesn't fall apart in a downpour of disappointment. It's an open ear that draws in all the thoughts and phrases without restricting what a person is allowed to say or think, and there is no judgment.

*Dolores Calley*

In my further education on trust, I came to doubt that trust is always earned. Wendel had taken money and items from the house. He had sneaked out of the house at night, attempted to kill himself, and had run away. This was not any reasonable person's vision of a trustworthy individual. During the climb up the mountain for both of us, I realized that regaining trust wasn't going to happen if I sentenced Wendel to a stint in "trust purgatory". If the two of us were going to build a bridge across the canyon that lay between us, Wendel and I both needed opportunities to reawaken a trust that had been, but had suffered abuse. Thus, I gave Wendel openings, small ones at first, buying items at the store, depositing money in the bank. And when I lost my sitter for Michael, sixteen-year-old Wendel's brother, I turned to Wendel as the interim baby sitter. Faith in Wendel's ability to rise out of the ocean of madness, combined with a loving desire to move into a better place with each other allowed a renewed sense of trust to develop quickly. This could only happen because Wendel truly got a clean slate, a new day, an opportunity to start fresh. Wendel gave me the same gift.

*Awakening Wisdom from Innocence*

I think that when major challenges present themselves in life, they often force reevaluation of the beliefs that have been held as a complete and unshakable code of living. Since these beliefs are exposed as incomplete and changeable through the hard experiences, a person may be left to stumble through uncharted territory and rebuild a new code of living. The path is seldom marked with signs that can be seen or recognized as familiar. When these moments come the individual is often left only with the choice to accept that something exists, exists beyond or very deep within human senses. These are the moments when faith truly develops or the individual begins to unravel. At the end of one's life when death comes, there is little more than faith that can be taken into the new beginning, so it is a worthwhile pursuit.

One needs not wait for death to begin this understanding. Each person can recognize his or her self as a priority and learn to trust. One can begin by accepting that there is personal benefit from the dramas in which life encourages participation. Once these two things are mastered, self as a priority and faith in the rightness of one's life, the individual can live life with a healthy openness and an innocent vulnerability. Children do this regularly by believing everything their father says and trusting that all of their mother's actions are right and based on love. Perhaps there is great wisdom in this combination of beliefs. All children come into this world having faith that they will be cared for, loved, and honored. Is their faith wrong or have we, as adults, long forgotten our own childhood truth? Maybe people spend much of their adulthood rediscovering what they already knew as a child.

For adults, the ability to gain from the wisdom of children only takes an open mind and respect for the child. Within families it is sometimes difficult to recognize or appreciate the value of some experiences. Compassionate detachment allows for objectivity. The additional insights available to those using an objective lens gives clarity to the role one has chosen in varying life dramas. It is also very important to NOT take any of the drama personally.

Now if the concept of family is expanded to encompass the society we live in, the priorities that children present for society to address can be reviewed. Along with recognizing what important things society may be putting on the back burner, an understanding of the dynamics and communication between adults and children can be realized. Are the adults reacting in a supportive manner and joining in partnership to work through the lesson, gain valuable insights through the experience, and adjust lives and beliefs so that greater harmony and peace can be shared by all within the society?

Recently, I went to a conference on rural education. A teacher from Vermont talked about a discussion in which teachers and students from her school had participated. At their meeting the adults asked the children how they thought they, as children, would be perceived by an adult stranger who passed them on the street. The students almost uniformly answered that the adult would think them lazy, unmotivated, uneducated, dangerous, and other negative attributes. The teacher said that they found similar results when they went to other areas of the country and asked the same question.

A second question was asked; how would you like to be perceived by an adult stranger? Students answered this question with comments such as smart, creative, capable, responsible, and other redeeming qualities. Obviously, the students are telling grown-ups something profound. The actual perception of today's children by adults is not aligned with the picture the children wish to share. They want a fair chance. They want adults to see an accurate picture, one that coincides with their own belief in themselves. They want to be respected participants. But they also feel that the average adult is not even giving them an opportunity; no fresh start, no clean slate, no trust.

Based on what the students put forth during this exercise, the adults said, "Okay, let's include the older children in on major decisions regarding our town." Amazing things happened. The adults found out that their kids were capable, sincerely concerned with the community, and full of fresh, creative ideas. The kids discovered that they could work with adults in an atmosphere of mutual respect. The youth found out that there really was something of significance they could share with adults. All it took was sharing community needs as a priority in partnership with younger members of the town, facing the vulnerability, and allowing trust without the traditional trust earned time period.

Not long ago I had an intense dream that falls right in line with this man-made abyss between the adults and children in western society. The atmosphere for me, as an adult in the dream, was one of mounting panic. In the dream I was alone in my mother's home. As I fluffed the bed pillow preparing to read, I couldn't get the lights on. I arose and went into the living room because I heard voices. The TV was throwing a ghastly light into the darkness of the room. No matter what I did, including pulling out the plug, I could not turn off the TV.

The phone rang and briefly distracted me. My mother was on the line, but I also noticed her knocking at the door, which was at the end of a long, dark corridor. At first I could speak into the phone, but as the conversation progressed, my words turned into a slow-speed garble, totally incomprehensible. As the panic rose to a crescendo, I woke up sweating.

I don't make a point of analyzing dreams, but this one really clicked. I felt that I had experienced as an adult and within a dream framework, the atmosphere of some children's lives. Imagine being little and during the week you see the adults, with whom you have bonded and now look to for care and love, only at breakfast, dinner, bath time, and bedtime. The rest of the time you are either sleeping or going to day care. You, as the young child, don't even really have an opportunity to turn on the light of love, communication, sharing, or understanding. As you get a little older, the TV serves as a companion before you go off to school, when you come home to an empty house, or maybe when your Mom's fixing dinner after a long day of work. Thus, there are lights that won't come on and a TV that cannot be turned off.

The end of the dream seems to illustrate how difficult communication can be when time together is penciled in on the calendar. Initially, there may be some quality time with the delightful, trusting toddler, but as these children grow, they learn to find family in the other people with whom they spend more time. As they grow into teenagers, they have grown away from their parents and closer to a family unit of friends or even a gang.

I admit that I have placed work and chores higher on the list than time spent with my children. I have snapped on the TV to get a break from parenting. I have felt wrenching guilt when doing this. So I do not point this out to make anyone feel badly. This is here so that individuals can look at how much or how little of a priority their children actually are within the family. The view can than expand to determine the priority of children within society. One can look at the situation objectively. One can view a larger picture. Each person can look at the picture that includes neighbors, fellow workers, and media coverage of children. Then each individual can evaluate society's general child rearing methods and the general adult attitude toward children. Having explored this perspective, one can then include the actions of children (suicide, violence, disrespect, etc.). At this point one has a basis to decide if changes need to be made in the family and/or the society with regard to children. This is an important decision because children do grow up and become important decision makers in the future. Children both reflect and contribute to the evolving health or illness of society's changing reality.

For example, one could look at American society's outlook on drugs. In addressing this issue as parents, one wants to look at what the children's actions are saying about cultural priorities. One also needs to examine adult response, and see if the society is growing through the experience, working in partnership with both adults and children, and making adjustments based upon the new insights gained from the experience.

*Dolores Calley*

Some people realize that, although schools teach children from second grade on that drugs are dangerous and bad for their health, many of the same children are drugged for inappropriate behavior at school. The use of Ritalin and other medications (Dexedrine, Adderall, Cylert, etc.) in the treatment of attention and focus problems in school has risen sharply over the last several years. Several million children are on treatment. Based on the rapidly increasing numbers, one can infer that children, by their behavior are indicating a major problem with focusing on schoolwork. Students have presented this as a priority for adults to look at. From this large jump in the use of this class of prescription drugs by school children, it becomes evident that the primary way society has chosen to deal with this problem is by drugging children to counteract the disruptive behavior in class. To explain the behavior problems at school, one could include other possibilities, such as a disease of the educational system, changes in birthing procedures, additives, inoculations, or other contributing factors when assessing this situation. The children may not be the cause.

One can also look at parental response to the school behavior issue. Is there a different way to address this problem? Also it might be enlightening to understand why the administration of drugs to children to encourage expected behavior was chosen. One might also want to consider why children are instructed about the dangers of drugs on one hand, and often subjected to drug therapy to resolve the problem of paying attention at school on the other hand. Generally, a powerful and accepted way to educate is by example, instead of resorting to "do as I say, not as I do."

Certainly society could have picked any number of different ways to address this situation; many individual families have done just that. For example, some families are working with alternative therapies, homeopathy, herbs, and diet modification. There is literature to support quite an array of successful outcomes without the use of the above-mentioned drugs. Other families have decided to adjust their lives. With one parent home full time, the parent can be more available either for home schooling or greater involvement in a public or private school. Another possibility may be enrolling the child in a private school. There is a much broader range of teaching and learning opportunities outside the public school system. Even though drug therapy dominates, there certainly are many other avenues available to address this problem. I have only illustrated a few.

The reason drug therapy has predominated appears to be multifaceted. Modern Western culture has become very dependent on drugs for any number of health issues. Everyone is waiting for a cure for cancer, AIDS, and other diseases. People have been conditioned to the cure from a little magic pill. Pills often alleviate symptoms but rarely eliminate disease. In the case of attention deficit disorders, eliminating the symptoms and modifying the behavior is the goal. Eliminating the source of the condition is rarely sought. In fact, the option of a complete recovery hardly exists as a plausible possibility.

The treatment generally does accomplish a change in behavior. So as a parent who has chosen the drug route, there will often be positive results. The child will often be rewarded with higher grades as he or she focuses on the task at hand. Just the other day I spoke with a high school student who has been on Ritalin for almost a year. He is very pleased, even though he has on occasion suffered from nausea, headaches, and mood swings, because his grades have gone

*Awakening Wisdom from Innocence*

from a 2.0 to a 3.8. I cannot argue with his success, but I can question the overall value of what he is learning and where he is heading. I can ask if the goal (a 3.8 average in school) is worth the major change in his being. I can be concerned about the long-term effects of drug therapy.

There was another young boy in my science class last year whose parents decided to choose drug treatment for their son's diagnosed ADD. This fellow was a delightful, social, happy guy, but the change to middle school was difficult for him. He was having a terrible time trying to keep all those teachers and their assignments in order. Thus, he often missed turning his homework in when it was due. After a meeting where he and his parents sat opposite five teachers and the vice principal discussing the young boy's lack of success and the severity of the situation, the lad was put on drugs for his attention deficit disorder. I find it strange that this condition waited to show up until the seventh grade. I vividly remember his dazed look after he started treatment, and I certainly missed his bubbly, happy smile. I never saw it again. I would have traded that smile for any homework assignment he handed in on time. As a parent, one may need to look at the information that is being used to evaluate the child's needs. Often the parent may be challenged to move beyond a quick fix. As of this moment, no one knows the ramifications of long-term drug usage on children for the treatment of attention deficit disorders.

In our country success is measured by how much money is made, not dedication to helping the community. Personal wisdom, honesty, and integrity are often valued less than money acquired at any and all costs. If financial success is the goal for children, the steps to follow to achieve it are laid out by the educational system, another major business. But I'm here to say some of the most creative and intelligent kids are unable to make it in an educational system that teaches cultural diversity and demands induced complacency and sameness, that teaches drugs are bad and dangerous but recommends their daily use for children, and that preaches family involvement in the school while digging for any stretchable weakness of the parents so that the child can be labeled "needy" and thus, provide more dollars to the school. Many of these outcast children go on to be very successful despite the educational system. If compliance and sameness are forced upon children, society looses this rich source of creativity and imagination. As the diversity in nature diminishes with the extinction of species, the rich diversity of being human is being lost by lack of faith and trust in childhood and apathy to a screaming segment of the population, the children.

The society's position on drugs is but one example; I could use the high rate of poor readers, teenage pregnancy, the rise of the gang culture, the amazing number of runaway or discarded children, school shootings, or another item off the list of disturbing trends seen in the younger population. Within each example, the message is clear. The children show adults that modern society, the current way of life is lacking, painful, and often inadequate for achieving happiness. All concerned people need to address this matter. Whether one makes changes as individual families or as a society, adults need to recognize their children, their family lifestyle, as a priority.

In the beginning of this chapter, I shared some personal lessons on priorities, trust, and vulnerability that have occurred because of my children. My children served as windows of opportunity to understand myself better, to uncover my own deep beliefs, and to adjust my code of living based on the valuable insights gained through the experiences often thrust upon me by John, Wendel, and Michael. Understanding the significant role that my children have played in helping me know myself better, I have gained a sense of awe in the amazing gift children are to all of us. Not only do they delight with their antics, love unconditionally, and bring laughter and music into their homes, they help adults remember from where they have come. Children, through their actions, also continue to question the way the society functions. Adult and child share the same heritage, childhood.

There is much talk about angels nowadays. Some people say that there are angels among us. I would agree. The angels are the children. For the children remain as teachers of spirit. Teaching about a greater reality of living and participating in the world that goes beyond our earthly experience, belongs almost exclusively to children. As adulthood is attained, each person commits to structure, the structure of society, work, economy, education, and all the other institutions and bureaucracy that direct the way people live. Children allow us the opportunity to once again experience life with the innocence of a greater wisdom based on vulnerability, tucked carefully in a nest of trust.

# Chapter 2

# Play, Focus, and Creativity

How do these little angels learn to function in their new world? At a very early age they seem to play their way through their days. Language bubbles forth, often in response to reactions from people received by the baby to gurgling and cooing. Often the baby's behavior seems to be used to invite grown-ups to join in the game. Infants learn quickly and become experts at engaging adults in play. I think baby talk, peek-a-boo, and pat-a-cake were developed by babies for adults. And adults seem to enjoy them, playing over and over, smiling, laughing, and acting silly, just like kids. This early play seems devoted to communication and interaction with people.

I know I looked forward to having children so that I would have an excuse to fly kites, play in the park, and feel young and excited when I visited Disneyland. Babies and toddlers give adults a chance to go back in time and play. As adults, people have traded precious playtime in for work. Children, once they start their formal

*Awakening Wisdom from Innocence*

education, get schooled in turning play into something productive, and that equals work. Look at the stress that can build up in half an hour in the workplace. How often does one find a stressed child at play? By exploring the world of play, one can see the loss an individual suffers because the play of childhood is exchanged for the stress of work in adulthood.

Picture a peaceful beach. The sea gulls are lazily calling overhead and the slap, lap rhythm of a gentle surf draws your own heartbeat into harmony with the cycle of waves falling upon the shore. Imagine you are with your child who wants to build a sand castle. Your initial reaction as you ponder with gratitude the refreshing escape from work, "Oh no, Mommy just wants to lay in the sun and rest. Maybe later."

Since I'm guiding this mind trip, get up and join your little one at the water's edge. Sit in the sand without a towel beneath your bottom (children never care about sand stuck in delicate places), feel the cool water running further and further up your legs. Forget the little mind comments about the beach walkers passing by. It is very important to put every other thing out of your mind because you are getting ready to play like a child. Ditch the adult mentality that goes through the motions of play while mentally making lists of things that need to be picked up at the supermarket, reviewing what chores need doing in the next day or two, and wondering how the stock market is doing. The goal (to satisfy you task oriented mind) is to leave the past and the future somewhere else in time and bring your complete attention into the present, the scene of a restful beach.

Remember you are safely tucked into a comfy chair so forget that your behind is much too big in that old bathing suit you are wearing and that you'll burn lobster red if you stay in the sun more than half an hour. Do not notice that the fellow coming down the beach in speedo trunks has a really nicely built body. See how many racing thoughts stuff themselves into the already overflowing crevices of our moments!

A wonderful bit of wisdom from the very tiny ones is to have a CLEAR MIND! Without a clear mind you cannot fully focus on the task or the pleasure at hand, realize the information signaling through your senses, or appreciate the "now" moment of your life. Many people have minds that overwhelm like the typical teenager's bedroom. The garbage is combined with the treasures in a heap that penetrates every corner. Unless you can achieve time with your child when you can shut the bedroom door of your mind, you'll only have a washed out illusion of that precious quality time the experts emphasize.

So sweep out the cluttered room and get back on the beach. You have some sand castle building to do. Now that your mind is free and peaceful, you can really notice the pure raw sensations that are all around you, the cool wetness of the sand, the waves of gentle caresses from the breeze, the tingling warmth of the sun and salt water on your skin, and the sweet song of your child's voice. After determining a perfect site for your castle and preparing the construction mixture, you and your child let the creation as well as the conversation move you along as it may. If something is not quite right, you change it, trying different things. There is no wrong or right way because the castle plans are being developed as you build. They are very flexible. If the sea comes in and washes a wall down, neither of you get upset. You interact with the environment, accepting it's place as you accept the air you breathe, adapting to it's changes as you flow with changes in the weather. Doesn't the harmony of the picture, the give and take of the play, feel amazingly peaceful and stress free?

You finish, and it surely is a good feeling. Together you admire your work and then your sweet little child gleefully dances over the castle. All that remains of the masterpiece is sand-sized pebbles that are slowly but surely reclaimed by incoming waves.

Within this daydream reality there are some simple, yet deep as the ocean truths about our world and the magnificent reflection of nature in which we all participate. Your child has served as the guide reminding you of those endless magical moments alone as a child when you accepted without thought, only a knowing, a simple faith in the order and rightness of life. For this brief time you have been able to live without the responsibility of making anything happen or the pressure of deciding what needs to happen in the future. This child guide, through the easy act of play, has given you the opportunity to focus and savor just the moment, but much more thoroughly than our daily routine permits. The order of our days, out of necessity, requires a constant comparison with the past and a constant establishment of plans for the future. We all procure money in some way to pay the bills that will unfailingly find their way into our mailboxes sometime in the future. The past, watching our parents go to work and having worked as a youngster ourselves, tells us having a job maintains the pattern of our society. And, heaven forbid, what would happen if the pattern changed or disappeared completely? Once we grow up we hardly ever turn off the incessant demands of the mind to relate and assess the present moment in light of the past and future. The children remind us that it is healthy to step away from these demands and restore ourselves with the easy pace of play.

Another major truth is all to evident at the end of the sand castle scene, and for some it is a little disturbing, uncomfortable. After all the fun of building the castle, your sweet angel dances it into the formless sand and surf that made the construction material. If you are annoyed at the destruction of the castle, you need to recognize and then rise above the frustration. Remember the larger perspective can be viewed if you detach and give up the personal affront (victim mentality). So what if the castle is gone. It was just a product of a lovely time shared with someone you love. Maybe the _process_ of building the castle and not the _product_ (the castle) was the really important part of this playful afternoon. Maybe you could have been riding bikes or baking cookies.

As for the castle or any other product, all things of this earth, including the bodies we like to believe belong to us, are made of recycled atoms and molecules that have been coming together, forming something new, and then drifting apart only to repeat the process over and over again for billions of years (and we thought we invented recycling). Even more outrageous is the fact that a little child had to engage you in a moment of play to demonstrate the awesome pattern of circles within circles that bring forth our experience of living.

Unfortunately, these natural cycles and an emphasis on the process instead of the product do not fit well with society's picture of life. Modern society is based on products, consumerism, big business, the stock market, and a global economy that we go to the ends of the earth to support. Think of how far you'd get if you told your boss that during the process of getting the new breakfast cereal out on the market, the group had an enlightening chat about life. So, even though a great marketing plan was developed, the group chose to toss the paperwork into the trash. Of course, the warmth and vision of the group sharing was priceless, and as a well-educated middle manager surely the boss appreciates the important things in life. I don't think so.

It is much more likely that when you say you are not coming in on Saturday because your son has a baseball game, and you have already put in ten unpaid hours of overtime during the week that you are met with some subtle reminder of how much you need this job. The reminder may even be followed up with a dose of reinforcement, "We hired you because you've got what it takes to get the job done." As you may agree, success in our society is product based, and consequently, short lived.

If you are hesitant, decide for yourself. Think a moment on these questions. Do you think that we, as a society, really accept death as an integral, significant part of life? Do we appreciate equally the contributions to our community that each age group has to offer? Do we readily remind ourselves through play that so often in life the process, not the product, has a far older history and a much broader impact? I bring up these examples because acknowledging the dichotomy between the play of youth and the work of adulthood encourages our own personal review. Then questions can be brought up about the effectiveness of society's methods and foundations. This is a time when adult linear thinking comes in real handy. Once you assess and compare, you can decide in a consciously aware manner how you want play and work to fit into your family life.

When I started teaching, people used to ask me if I really enjoyed teaching first graders. There was a feeling that I must be bored having to reach so far back into my own development. But I have to tell you that I found first graders intensely interesting, much more open-minded, creative, and unique when compared to seventh graders or many adults with whom I have worked. What I was concurrently learning in my education theory classes hardly scratched the surface of what I was experiencing with these delightful little people. One young lad could see and create intricate patterns. As the year progressed he repeated this in math, language arts, and science. He began to relate the different patterns to each other and displayed a solid understanding of systems thinking. Although I never read about it in any educational theory book, I realized his style of learning was

*Awakening Wisdom from Innocence*

based on his ability to recognize patterns and their relationships. This all came about from his own creative play, not my instruction. Another girl was often instructing other students, puppets, kittens. She sorted information by passing it along to a creative array of audiences. Here I was working, producing students who could read, write, and calculate, and the children were learning so much in their own unique ways from their play. The year was enjoyable, because I too, was able to play. I sang songs, sat in a circle on the floor sharing stories, and exchanged many heartfelt hugs. Within the classroom the children and I found a good balance of play and work.

One reason why children, especially the very young, do play so well is because of their ability to focus very intensely. I always thought how bizarre it must be to fall asleep in one place and wake up in another. Infants do this regularly, and it doesn't seem to bother them at all. My explanation to myself for this strange phenomenon is that the infant focuses so much in the present that each moment is magical and new and relative to nothing, quite the opposite of the adult scattered focus, which compares unfamiliar experiences to previous knowledge. The baby seems to respond to the environment he finds himself in without any expectations. There are no preconceived notions, because the infant has not amassed a wealth of environments or experiences with which to compare new things. She is free to explore and has nothing but her own creativity to guide the experience. The adults who share life with the child are established in their own way of experiencing life, and thus, unable to relate in any but a most superficial way to the infant's world.

I know how I would respond if I went to bed at night and woke up in China with some strange, giant humans, uttering sounds, and making gestures and varying facial expressions. I know I'd totally panic and start up the old mind conversation. "What on earth is going on here? This place is weird. Where are my buddies, my family, my life? Help, help, please let this just be a little nightmare!"

Yet, if one looks at infancy only from a mature, linear pattern of assessing experiences, comparing something new to previous information, it's amazing that babies can function at all. Not only do they seem completely capable of making their needs known, they learn about us and how things are within the family. Actually, the most intense period of learning and skill acquisition occurs well before any one of us has stepped through the esteemed portal of a classroom.

Have you ever watched an infant reaching for something or learning to crawl? They really focus on what they want to accomplish. Over and over a baby will reach and try to grasp for the object. The little one will be tenacious in his efforts and suffer no apparent disappointment at attempts that fall short of the object. He will just continue until the goal is achieved. The baby keeps working at it, focusing deeper and deeper, pushing the limits of his previous efforts until his little hand wraps around the object. Same thing with crawling. She will push up and rock, stretching out a hand, moving a knee until she reaches that new and interesting place in the room. There is an intense focus that is determined by the child's curiosity and interest. During the child's early development, the parent, as well as the wee one, trust that he or she will recognize and work on what he or she needs to learn in order to participate. The first eighteen months of each of our lives is filled with major milestones. Babies learn to sit up, feed themselves, move about on their own, recognize loved ones, communicate through language, and ever so many more things.

My little guy Michael illustrated this focused, self-directed way of learning to me even after he started kindergarten. He enjoyed playing on the computer, and he wanted to read so that he could do more things on the computer. For more than six weeks, Michael spent an hour or two a day on the computer working with some early reading software I had for him. Occasionally he asked me to read a word, but he worked almost exclusively on his own. For Michael this was fun, and he had determined his own purpose. Being young and still close to all the baby learning, he approached his desire with determination and no thought of failure.

In the seventh week I said, "Okay Michael, let's read a book." We started out with an early reader, one with a word or simple sentence on each page, but quickly traded it in for a much more difficult book. Michael was able to read *The Giving Tree*, by Sol Silverstein with very little help. This book is challenging for the average first or second grader. Michael had achieved that level of

*Awakening Wisdom from Innocence*

reading ability in seven weeks, alone on a computer, because he wanted to and because he focused on acquiring the skill.

In a school atmosphere where there is a high percentage of children reading below grade level, Michael's accomplishment was looked upon with awe and doubt. This reaction occurred because adult linear thinking is plagued with limitations. Educators could hardly accept the fact that I had little to do with Michael's newly developed reading ability. Somehow the skepticism worked out well for both of us. As Michael moved into first grade, I also joined the first grade staff at his school as a part-time teacher. Michael's achievement undoubtedly boosted my consideration for employment.

Now John had presented a very different situation. I was told, on more than one occasion, that John had a learning disability, an attention problem at school. I knew that this same little boy who seemed so distracted to his teachers could spend hours with Lego blocks or balsa wood creating an endless array of contraptions. Maybe the difference for John was playing instead of working. Maybe John was determined to follow his own heart's desire and put off "work" for as long as possible.

John, through play, had done some wonderful things. Memories of him as a child include not only blown fuses and black stripes running up the wall from the outlets, but also beautifully crafted wooden floating boats and precisely made models. The balsa wood boats were created from the pictures in his mind. It always amazed me that this six-year-old boy could think of something he wanted to build, cut out the pieces, which usually fit perfectly the first time, and set a unique boat that floated into the water. In his play, John was determining for himself how the world was put together. At school John was always a struggling student, but in his creative world of play John was a master at understanding how things work. Today, as an adult, John is a capable carpenter, electrician, and handyman, but he has no licenses stating that he had learned these trades.

My boys have given play a new meaning for me. They have thoroughly enjoyed the process of playing. I can hear the sound effects and see them leaping through the air, crashing to the floor, totally into their own little reality. They never seemed to worry about the outcome. I've often heard or seen them go back, repeat the scene, and end on a very different note. There seems to be an extraordinary freedom in doing something with no need to reach a goal or produce a product. Without the stress of an anticipated outcome, the process holds the focus and carries the information. Stress builds once the process of creating is tied to an outcome.

Disappointment, self-doubt, and failure become part of a socialized human being once someone is assessing and judging the progress. The formal introduction into these destructive aspects of being human generally begins in school. Sure there is a traditional transition period in kindergarten, but then report cards, routine assessment, and standardized tests let the child, and everyone else, know how he or she stacks up. The focus changes. With increased pressure to produce, the children begin to tie their worth to the products of their brainpower, so much so that even drugs will be taken to increase their success.

Encouraging the young child to believe his or her worth is directly related to his or her mental function and ability to inevitably produce marketable goods or services serves the philosophy of a capitalistic society very well. The real question is, does it serve the individual, and consequently, the society, in a healthy, harmonious manner? To find the answer one needs to explore the potential of childhood to encourage familiarity and understanding about the process of living. By observing children one can quickly realize that the partnership of play and focus most often blossoms in the realm of creativity. Once the grown individual explores the attributes of creativity, he or she can decide consciously whether real creativity is most effective producing an endless stream of new products that eventually pile up and obstruct the river of life or change the present practice to increase support for the development of the expanded creative expression illustrated by children.

True creativity is the budding horticulturist who believes she can communicate with the plants. It is John, the boat designer, who cannot do the math required for an engineering degree. It is the Wright brothers showing a less structured world that man can fly. True creativity sleeps in all the seemingly outrageous, impossible dreams that have been discarded because individuals need to be sensible and find their way in the "real world." Now, tell me where the "real world" is. Does it live in the economy driven, big Monopoly game of life or in the magnificent potential of our unrestricted dreaming?

In the process of play, as portrayed by the child and done with intense focus in the present moment, creativity is awakened. The curiosity that encouraged the creativity, gives self-expression free reins and unlimited access. The lack of limitation is an important item here. When is the last time any adult did not have a really long line of limitations (they are usually called responsibilities) awaiting their turn at restricting something someone really wanted to at least try. Maybe that is why people often die feeling like they never really lived.

An enlightened moment about the unhappy relationship between the creativity of play and the restriction of limitations came to me in a dream. Michael, as the young lad he is, and I were playing outside. He was busy in a lower field climbing up ladders into the bottom branches of a tree. I was on top of the hill. The two of us were happy and laughing.

At some point I was distracted and looked into a mirror at my teeth. I had five very ugly looking metal teeth, but way in the back of my mouth there was one tooth that was gold and sparkling. Overall I felt that it was a pretty shoddy dental job, but I had a sense of acceptance; the teeth functioned well.

When I went back to the edge of the hill to check on Michael, he had dragged over a very tall, wooden ladder. He was already nearing the top of the ladder, peeking at me from between the green leaves. As I looked beyond his smiling face at the ground so far below, I panicked.

"Michael, get down off that ladder! You're up far too high," I ordered. "And you be very careful getting down."

His little face crumpled. I could see my own fear overtake him as he began to descend with the utmost of caution. The sturdy wooden ladder immediately started to give way, rapidly turning into a swaying, bending mass of hoses.

Being a dream the scene shifted, and I was watching a car pull up to my woodpile on the back of my property. A couple of young men jumped out of the car and grabbed pieces of wood. Filled with anger at their blatant theft, I yelled at them. They dove back into the car and sped away flashing badges at me as they passed. The badges were used to somehow exonerate their reprehensible actions.

They slowed and pulled the car around to where I was standing. Both of them got out of the car and explained how they needed the extra money the wood would bring to pay for their mortgages and other expenses. They also said they were sorry and knew what they were doing was wrong. At that point, I not only forgave them, but also completely accepted and understood their behavior. Their admission of sorrow and the recognition of the inappropriateness of their actions was enough for me to dismiss the incident altogether.

The message in this dream was fairly obvious. As long as Michael did not exceed a height I found acceptable, I could laugh and play with him. Once he started climbing higher into the tree, I set a limitation, telling him he wasn't allowed to go that high. He accepted my boundary, lost his focus, and the ladder of creativity and exploration collapsed into a pile of fear and self-doubt.

Now, the teeth are an interesting and meaningful symbol for me, but perhaps not everyone. I believe that teeth are related to personal beliefs, and as beliefs change, teeth can indicate new awareness or the need for awareness. Most of my teeth in the dream, when viewed by me, came down to being a "pretty shoddy job," but functional. There was one beautiful tooth in the area of the wisdom teeth, symbolic of what all the teeth (beliefs) could be if I pushed beyond functionality, maturing into an expanded viewpoint based on wisdom.

How, you ask, do the thieving cops fit in with the rest of the dream? They are grown men with the trappings of adult life (mortgages). Although I restricted Michael's play, setting distinct boundaries, I came to accept the lame excuse for the adult behavior of the cops, even when I clearly knew they were wrong. Isn't this often true of adults? Grown-ups often circle kids like hawks waiting for them to slip up, to venture out into the open space. As soon as the children cross the boundary, adults usually pounce on them with the full force of seniority power. At the same time, adults back away or cover up inappropriate grown-up behavior with a healthy layer of rationalization. Once again the dichotomy of the adult world and the reality of the child line up on opposite sides of the field. Maybe adults just lose their creativity in the static of every day life. Thus, the older generation teaches restrictive limits to children, while forgiving the weaknesses of those they identify with, other adults. After all, any one of us adults might succumb to similar temptation and need an excuse along with support from our peers.

I also find it interesting that the symbol of wood is tied into both the scene with Michael and the two policemen. For Michael it is the ladder that forms his bridge to creativity and exploration, and it crumbles under the weight of fear and self-doubt. The cops, on the other hand, are stealing wood. They use the wood to get money, and the money goes to support the trappings of modern day life. So one can see the creativity of their childhood has been compromised. Now their creativity is useful only as a means to supply the material things in their lives. This once unlimited creativity has been reduced to solving the problems presented by the confining dictates of society. The adult creativity finds purpose in devising new ways to acquire material possessions, not satisfy the heart's desire to serve the world with the individual's unique beauty.

Two years ago I would have referred you to my younger sister, the artist, if you asked me about creativity in my family. I felt that I didn't have a creative bone in my body. In my eyes, I was very capable of mental exercises, household chores, and family obligations, but creative, no way.

The year as a teacher in first grade ignited a small smoldering fire within me just waiting to burst into flames. A person does not face twenty eager little faces every day without a plan, and if I wanted to count on keeping them engaged and busy, I had better have a creative plan. Remember, I had more opportunity to play and explore my own creative abilities in that year than I probably had in any other year of my whole life. And those twenty little teachers were masters at play. So, we sang to the garden to make the plants grow, and when they did, we used them in our chicken soup. Together we constructed a child-sized scarecrow and had a ceremony to place him in his new home. After writing plays we made costumes and props and performed for each other. I found a treasure trove of fun and educational things to do. To my surprise and delight, the ideas often came from my very own mind.

Finding myself teaching seventh grade science the following year definitely tested all I had learned from the instructors in first grade. With a budget of less than $2.00 a year per student for science

*Awakening Wisdom from Innocence*

supplies and no individual science books, there is little to rely on except creativity. Fortunately, I was able to do a lot with baking soda, vinegar, and one good microscope. Having been there, I marvel at the creativity of students and teachers. Creativity almost single-handedly separates the exciting classrooms from the stale, boring ones. Since children generally place higher on the creativity scale, there is probably a lot of student input sparking the excitement in those exceptional classrooms.

Recently, in my state as well as many others, new standards (requirements for skills a child at grade level needs to acquire) are being adopted into the curriculum at all grade levels. Along with the standards, there is a resurgence of the 3 "Rs", more drill and less hands on work. I recognize a need for better education, but it would be ever so refreshing to see society really think this issue through before making decisions. Instead, educators and politicians jump on one thing and treat the children like ping-pong balls being passed back and forth between the paddles of fashionable theories of education and politically expedient education decisions. Along with the standards, there is a call for mandatory preschool. This adult-structured play would bring an even earlier introduction to stress, self-doubt, and all the other limits restricting the youthful creativity of preschoolers.

Perhaps now is a good time to revisit play with one of the excellent teachers available. Once you clear your mind, find your way into an exclusive present, and push the creativity limits as far as possible beyond your usual comfort level, you are in for a treat. Before you add your stamp of approval, either through complacency or ignorance, to the pending government dictates for your children, you should explore their world. Aside from some authentic quality time with your children, who reflect the history and future of your family, you may really enjoy a stress free visit to some of life's great truths.

# Chapter 3

# Potential, Intuition, and Adaptation

What happens to these creative little beings, who have a clear mind and a powerful focus, as they grow? As the little one moves about the new world, the focus is intense with few distraction or points of comparison to previous knowledge. Exploration is self-initiated and directed with great intensity. Their work is done in a field that does not recognize failure. The learning system employed by the young child is an internal one, unique to the individual, and it has a proven track record of skill development and knowledge assimilation. During the life span of each being, he or she will never encounter another learning system that will even come close to being equal in efficiency to this early one. The capable, confident individual I speak of is a mere toddler.

Please pause for a moment and consider where people would presently be in their lives if these natural talents and abilities had been encouraged and supported by older community members. Go a little further and savor the excitement of working with others who expressed and shared their full potential in each present moment. Think of the harmonious and well-balanced world in which humanity could be living. A full manifestation of this incredible potential is very difficult to imagine, because each of us has traveled the road of growing up in modern western society. The road is pitted with limitations and judgments. There is a constant mist to force questioning and doubt as the individual takes each courageous step forward struggling with societal demands and suppression of the natural internal drive and curiosity. Add to this a forest canopy that is so dense very little sunlight touches the ground upon which the youngsters are treading. The journey continues as the child moves through the darkness of unknowing (ignorance of societal expectations), relying on the advice and direction of adults. If the natural trusting state of the young is somewhat intact, the individual is aware and fortified by the unseen forces that assist him or her.

Often the same engaging infants and endearing toddlers emerge from this forest of growth as sullen, resentful teenagers or angry, rebellious young adults; some remain lost in immaturity. Many of

*Awakening Wisdom from Innocence*

them have already explored the paths of escapism, drugs, alcohol, meaningless sex, and endless TV. Escape by it's very meaning says, "I am not going to solve the problems I encounter; I am not going to accept the challenges I face. Instead, I am going to avoid them and focus my energy on establishing new and more effective ways to remain in the darkness."

If one looks at potential, the energy that drives creativity, as a spiral, there are only two options. The potential can either twist tighter and tighter upon itself, or it can spiral ever wider, reaching into infinity. The choice is determined by either resolving problems and flowing into a new level or moving away from issues and allowing the energy outside of the spiral to exert a pressure that forces tighter and tighter circles. The downward spiral is finite, eventually closing in on itself until a roving black hole sucks it up, transforms the energy, and spits it out into a new place where the potential can start fresh. This process is destructive. The upward spiral is infinite, reaching outward through an ever-broadening circle of exploration. This process is creative.

*Dolores Calley*

Infants, by their very nature, work with the upward flow. Their desire to communicate stimulates the direction that leads them to solve problems, one after another, moving ever closer to their goal. One example is verbal exchange. Initially, they have the desire and through trial and achievement, they learn how to gain the attention of others in their world. Once an older person is cajoled into interaction, the next hurdle arises. What do I do to keep this person engaged? The infant experiments and finds that gurgling, cooing, and smiling work very well. These techniques even bring a response. The older person utters strange sounds, even ones that are repeated. Next stumbling block: how do I make these sounds, and what do they mean? One step at a time, the infant expands his ability to work with language, a major component of communication. The acquisition of language for the infant becomes a matter of overcoming a challenge and moving on to the next challenge, mastering that and repeating the procedure until the skill is incorporated into his or her very being.

When Wendel was struggling in his self-made sea of despair, he was definitely riding a downward spiral, caught in a swirling, mad whirlpool. This whirlpool, composed of Wendel's personal vision of his life, was extremely complete and terrifying. Wendel's creativity had included the raging, foamy waters that can bring death, and the powerful pull of the downward spiral into the whirlpool. The display resounded with an awesome potential for creativity, and this was the destructive side, the close-ended portion. If Wendel were to choose to redirect this creative force within him and start spiraling upward, he could easily realize the essence of the extraordinary within his lifetime. And he could do it again and again as he flung the circle ever wider. Happily, he is working on this, and the achievements of his early twenties have been remarkable.

Within each individual is the same kind of potential. This potential manifests in many ways as it yearns for greater and ever widening expression. Everyone has them, the dreams of what he or she might have done or would have like to try. Personally, I have been talking about writing a book for twenty-five years. Until I recognized and believed in my own creativity (a gift from the first graders), I did not have the confidence to take the risk and write. I had limited my potential in the area of creativity by what I believed was possible. There are many bits and pieces of unfulfilled creative potential stashed in the minds and hearts of people. Hidden away, this potential, which yearns to serve, must seek other expression. Maybe this lost potential finds life in inappropriate emotional response, physical disease, or the secret life of abuse.

On occasion, the world has been lucky enough to house someone who simply cannot suppress his or her potential. These individuals often redirect the course of humanity. Sometimes the price they pay is high, including ridicule, suffering, and even death. They carry this heavy burden because they are compelled to exercise their innate right to express the creativity they carry in the very essence of their being. Certainly, there have been many documented lives filled with torment because their vision would not submit to a societal call for the repression of their unique belief. Why is a new and different viewpoint so threatening to society?

Jesus Christ effectively brought the immense power of love to our planet. Although he had a following, the society of the time tortured and crucified him for living and sharing the beliefs in his heart. Other visionaries who called for change and who had followings, such as Malcolm X, Martin Luther King, John and Robert Kennedy, William

*Awakening Wisdom from Innocence*

Wallace, the witches of Salem, and others, were murdered or tormented by a societal structure unwilling to change. Socrates and Aristotle were both convicted for their ideas, the expression of their creative potential. Believing man could fly, the Wright brothers were ridiculed, and Nikola Tesla died penniless even though his creative insight has served as the basis for much of our modern technology. In his early years, Einstein had trouble finding work as a professor because of his radical thinking. Gandhi spent time in prison and was later killed because of his conviction and expression of passive resistance.

Still, the people cited above, along with many others, spiraled upwards following their internal drive and allowing their potential to manifest their unique creativity. Even when faced with adversity, they either could not or would not repress the growth of the seed, the vision within. By nourishing the seed with exploration and action, these men and women have at times profoundly affected society. They have often blazed trails and planted seeds of belief in the communal human psyche for those who followed.

*Dolores Calley*

Sometimes infants or children give grown-ups remarkable hints of the forgotten or suppressed abilities inherent in all human beings. Instinct houses a group of abilities with which a species is born. The suckling instinct of an infant is a commonly accepted instinct, but I believe there are many more. My dear Michael, as an infant, toddler and then youngster gave me some extremely powerful lessons in "instinctive" healing.

My background is in Medical Technology, so obviously, I have been well schooled in our western medical practices. Years in the same profession allowed me to see the shortcomings as well as the strengths. When my doctor strongly recommended I have a hysterectomy, I decided to try some alternative healing, and it served me well. During this time I worked with a woman whose healing methods included homeopathy. Through my work with her I was able to stave off anemia for a few years even though I bled very heavily each month.

At the age of forty-two, I found out that I was pregnant with Michael. Because of my age and the large fibroid tumor in my uterus, I was termed a high-risk pregnancy. The doctor had many concerns about going ahead with the pregnancy. I, trusting woman that I am, figured that since I was pregnant, apparently I was meant to be pregnant, and everything would turn out fine. To help insure the pregnancy would move along smoothly, I continued with the homeopathy. Since I was taking homeopathic remedies, Michael was also exposed to them as he grew in my womb.

I give the background information because the following illustration, of what I believe to be one of a number of significant human instincts, is still pretty incredible to me. Had I not had the lessons in trust from John and Wendel, this opportunity from Michael to join him in an exciting facet of healing may have had a very different outcome.

Michael was about five months old when he first showed me his amazing healing ability. Please remember I had devoted a large part of my life to contemporary medical diagnosis and treatment. Thus, Michael's healing talent came at me from somewhere beyond left field. On more than one occasion I saw Michael, a baby, restore his own health, but he did it so much more efficiently then anything I had previously encountered in the world of medicine. For Michael it was as natural as sleeping or eating. Even though it seemed impossible by present standards of medicine, I allowed it to be and validated the talent in Michael by cautiously accepting it. By withholding judgment I was able to watch and see where Michael was going with this ability.

The first time I saw this miracle, Michael was very sick, restless, crying, red-faced, and running a temperature of 103.5 F. In a panic I called my friend, the homeopathic healer. She listened to the symptoms and said, "I really feel that you already have the remedy you need."

I rapidly gathered up all the little vials I had in the cupboard. Since I was wearing a nightgown, I put all of them (about 35 bottles) in my skirt. Sitting down on the couch next to Michael, I hesitantly asked, "Michael, will any of these help you?"

Truly, I was skeptical, and I felt ridiculous. To my amazement he reached his little hand into the jumble of amber vials and pulled out a bottle.

"He picked out Stramonium, 1M," I called into the phone.

There was a pause and then, "That'll work."

"Wait, he's taking out another one," I said. "It's the same thing!"

"He seems to know what he wants. Go ahead. Give him some."

"But how much should I give him?"

The chuckle affirmed the smile I felt coming through the phone. "Since he obviously knows what he needs, I think we can count on Michael to know how much to take."

Forty minutes later my baby was sleeping peacefully. The fever was gone, and it never returned. Michael did this over and over again when he was sick. Even when he had a fever of 105 F, I trusted in his instinct. During each episode, once the fever left, and this always occurred in less than an hour, it never came back. As he repeated his success in restoring balance and health to his body, I was reassured and became more secure in my faith in Michael's instincts.

Michael has had strep throat, ear infections, and his share of fevers. He has always made the final decision on what remedy he wanted to take. His manner of healing has been in his hands since he was five months old. As far as conventional medical treatment, he has never taken antibiotics, and he has only had Tylenol once at a baby sitter's home.

*Dolores Calley*

This instinct, the ability to recognize what is needed to heal the body, is not unique to Michael. I have seen or heard about other young children just as adept as Michael. To my way of thinking, all individuals possess this ability to some degree. Unfortunately, in modern society one learns very early in life to hand over the responsibility of treating disease to a physician. People do this because the physician has studied the human body and disease states for many years. He or she has a degree and a license. Once a person chooses to hold the physician in higher regard than inner knowing, his or her own self-healing instinct remains dormant. Since Michael was supported and encouraged to take responsibility and exercise his natural inclination and right to maintain a healthy body, he was able to take this ability to a different level and help other people.

On several occasions Michael has spontaneously helped an injured friend. Between the ages of three and five years, he has walked over to someone that is hurt and said, "I can take away the pain." And he did. This is a beautiful example of moving upward in the spiral of potential. Michael moved from his personal healing to helping others. It could occur because of the support from people

*Awakening Wisdom from Innocence*

who were willing to exchange judgment for insight into an occurrence they didn't fully understand. Even though I had nothing to compare Michael's healing too, I withheld judgment and waited to see the results. Since the knowledge was new, continued exploration required openness on the part of myself and others. And Michael, having been given the go ahead, continued to expand the circle, moving to the next level in the spiral.

When Michael was six, my cousin Cathie came for a visit. She had only recently been diagnosed with Multiple Sclerosis (MS). Due to the illness Cathie was unsteady on her feet and unable to carry a cup of coffee from her kitchen to her dinning room. I asked Michael if he would check a remedy for Aunt Cathie. He choose one that felt "really good". The next morning my cousin buzzed past me with two cups of coffee. She carried them outside, down the step, and unto the deck. For two days her illness was gone, and Cathie was given the hope of knowing her body was capable of being restored to health. Cathie was inspired to see a doctor of homeopathy near her home. This new doctor started her on a much lower dosage of the same remedy recommended by six-year-old Michael.

Careful observation gave hints to other potential paths for this skill. An interesting aspect to Michael's direct involvement in his own healing occurred when I tried to give him fluoride drops for his teeth. As a baby, the homeopathic remedies were administered two ways, either drops in his cup or bottle or small sugar pills coated with the remedy. On absolutely every occasion I put the fluoride drops into the bottle Michael was drinking from, he tossed the bottle aside and refused to drink from it again. Something within must have told Michael that these drops were not healthy for him.

Today there is a lot of controversy surrounding the fluoridation of community water supplies. Fluoride in relatively low doses is extremely toxic to the human body. Although there seems to be evidence that fluoride helps prevent cavities, some communities have voted to keep fluoride out of their water supply. Evidence also suggests that fluoride causes an increase in broken bones. There is also some question about fluoride's reaction with other drugs, possibly contributing to suppression of mental abilities and physical stamina. Based solely on one baby's instinctive reaction to his fluoride drops, I am not surprised to see that years later the use of fluoride is being questioned.

What other wonderful instincts may be sleeping under the covers of our common beliefs? If, as parents and older, wiser adults, we can learn to temporarily withhold judgment, much less totally kill the unusual childhood behavior with ridicule and punishment, the mature segment of society may find themselves successfully uncovering treasure after treasure of gifts that have been carefully stored in a toy box in the attic of humanity. Relating Michael's innate talent back to primitive people gives greater sense to the presence of forgotten instincts in humans. The survival of primitive man would definitely have relied on a way to sort out healthy substances from deadly ones to ensure continued existence. What could be more efficient than an inner knowledge given as a gift from the natural world? Michael's instinct, which suggests awesome human potential, is supported by the indigenous cultures of today who offer a similar scenario.

For quite a few years, pharmaceutical companies have been going to the rain forests and native peoples seeking cures for diseases. There is a push to discover and preserve native plants and tribal remedies as both are growing increasingly rare with the expanding desire for land to support a rapidly growing world population and the need for a greater market of consumers. Perhaps individuals are also acknowledging that the instinctive wisdom of these simpler communities may hold the key to medical mysteries that have not yet been solved.

I'm sure that the cultural wealth of scientific knowledge has had little impact on either Michael's instincts or the remedies developed by isolated native cultures. Yet, many people will cling to the scientific method and the words of experts, allowing no room for obviously very effective alternative healing methods that have withstood the test of time. When a tiny candle flicker of light suggests there may be a bit of wisdom from a simpler source, western capitalists rush in like stampeding elephants. Their mission is to find the substance, analyze it, remake it, and call the compromised copy their own. Once the substance has been stripped down and rebuilt in an altered, marketable fashion, the "man made" stamp can be put in place and a patent will insure an exclusive right to manufacture. Soon to follow is the market development, the rationalized need, and the price tag. In a word, the corporate machine can then direct the adaptation.

The adaptive abilities of animals in their native environments are well known. Just recall the skin tones of the chameleon that adjust to the varying colors of its surroundings, or the bear's long sleep in response to the extreme cold and scarcity of food that comes with winter. Human beings have taken adaptation to a new and strange level. Maybe this is how people have distanced themselves from their instincts; the internal knowing that allows appropriate reaction to changes in the <u>natural</u> world. In the modern, technical world, people create the environment instead of adapting to the world in which they find themselves. People have learned how to control the presence of light, temperature, food selection, work, and entertainment activities, but recently, people are being reminded that the natural world holds the authentic power. People may try to convince themselves that they are in control, but the truth is that humans are an animal species and part of the natural world. For quite some time humanity has been allowed to play domination, but lately Mother Nature seems to be telling us to put the toys away and get real.

Infants, by virtue of their newness in the world, are extremely adaptable. Science has even uncovered information that shows there are many more open pathways in the brain of an infant than that of the adult. So, as the infant develops into a child, choices are made and certain options within the brain are shut down. From one study, it has been suggested that, although a person may learn a foreign language later in life, he or she may never be able to master certain sounds required to speak the language as a native. As a young child the language pathways for life were established through the early usage, and the pathways needed to "speak like a native" in a second language have either been established or shut down.

As the baby is exposed to the environment, he or she learns to adapt. Now science is even supporting the behavioral adaptation with actual physical changes taking place in the brain. Initially, the adaptation proceeds along the infant's natural inclinations, but as the child grows older, the adults and corporate machinery in society subtly guide adaptation.

Since, in western society, people have chosen to direct the collective energy into creating a world separate from the natural world, the child must be taught to adapt to the cultural experience. Herein lies the strangeness of human adaptation. Instead of responding to the world given humanity by the earth and nature, children are taught to respond and adapt to the cultural belief in controlling the environment and natural forces of the living space they share. Thus, our adaptation centers around adjusting the natural abilities with which we are born to accepting and functioning in an artificial environment under the control and dictates of people and their fascination with the technological manipulation of form and energy. All too often this adaptation necessitates the denial of inner wisdom and confusion about the individual's place in the natural order of things. Because the inner potential is powerful, the growing individual wastes all too much time trying to resolve a conflict that has very little chance of a harmonious outcome in the world structured by human beliefs in their artificial environment. Some of those who cannot resolve this attempt suicide, others seek alternatives—communes, co-housing, tribes, gangs, or "die" inside, adapt, and become human robots.

*Dolores Calley*

The toys given to the young to play with replace the rocks, trees, and other wonders of the natural world. Instead, little worlds are recreated out of plastic, and cute, happy-faced figures inhabit them. The experience of a nature hike takes the form of an adventure, sitting on the couch, munching on chips, watching a nature video on TV, and seeing nature up close and ever so comfortably, but not interacting with nature. The child is adapting; TV, the great culture-teaching tool is exerting itself as a necessity and plastic is beginning to feel more familiar than dirt. A life of consumerism is being established. The foundation of life in an artificial environment has been laid.

School serves as the next major stimulus for adaptation. In the early grades students learn to quietly sit in neat little rows and to arrange themselves in tidy lines with shoulder behind shoulder and head behind head. The child, still fresh with sensitivity for the world around him begins to get a message that will unfold slowly. This message speaks of what the adults do and what they value, hard work and good behavior. Gummy bears and stickers reinforce the display of appropriate behavior and developing work habits.

*Awakening Wisdom from Innocence*

At first, if the child's experience has been one of family support, love, and security, the child responds with joy and excitement at the prospect of beginning the initiation into the world of adulthood. Generally, they want to learn the secrets of the mature world and, by nature, are ready to cooperate and work with others. The faith and trust that carried them into this world and supported them well in their early endeavors are given away, given to the teacher without a moment's hesitation.

As they move through the grades, the happy little scenes of kindergarten fade away, because superimposed over the lessons of proper behavior and hard work, the child begins to understand failure, judgment, competition, and that the ends justify the means. All too often internal conflict develops because of the dichotomy of school-structured learning and the early self-directed learning. Sometimes the child, with his or her actions, says, "I don't want to adapt!" The sad fact is that once the "bad" behavior starts, the child has acquired a label that will fill his or her path with stumbling blocks, redirecting the child on a course that continues to reduce any chance of success within the system.

*Dolores Calley*

I think there is a profound message from the young people in the capitalistic world contained in that emphatic statement. The children show all who will carefully observe that the structure of society has become too rigid, heavy, and restrictive. Since their early self-directed way of solving problems and expanding the circle fueled by their own creative potential is still engaged within their scope of learning, they can approach our very structured, fact-based teaching with a keener, more objective eye. Many of them are rejecting what the established adult world has to offer. Adults need to heed the message of the youth in society if they, as creators of society, want to open up the gates of human potential and allow inner guidance to show people the way out of some very destructive corners into which society members have wedged themselves. The solutions, upon which human survival depends, may well be bound in the message of the children, the experience of childhood, which each person has lived, and the wisdom of the diminishing "primitive cultures." For example, how many individuals spend much of their adult lives sorting through the experiences of their childhood? Perhaps this is at the direction of inner knowing, indicating that one has not learned and

*Awakening Wisdom from Innocence*

put into practice the wisdom of their own innocence. The internal guidance is showing the individual where to find the answers.

This rejection of the current system of education by students is not new. The subtle messages of John and Wendel's generation have become clearer over the years. So often, if the hints are not recognized and the problems unresolved, the indications escalate to a point where they can not be ignored. The present society no longer just deals with high drop out rates and low-test scores, we now see long-term suspensions from school, school shootings, teen suicide, and other sorrows of modern youth. Perhaps these are echoes of the cry, "I don't want to adapt." Perhaps this statement pleads for healthy change.

Banning kids from school via suspension does not address the issue of educating them. The problem only worsens because, even when denied, the creative potential exists. The constructive avenues of outlet for this drive become more limited, more difficult for the disruptive child to find, less supported by the community, and subject to further entanglement in criminal or destructive activities.

One interesting attempt by the schools to address this problem of adaptation is to teach "anger management" in some form or other from the very early grades on up. The human emotional system is on a par with the intelligence of the mind. They are equivalent in complexity and multiple organ system input. Asking the emotional nature to conform to a logical thinking framework is like asking one's reproductive system to digest food. These systems are to work in partnership, each performing their own function for the benefit of the whole, not yield to domination by a partner system.

If I react emotionally to something, I feel it. I do not think it. Consequently, a lot of logical steps to objectively work through an emotional experience deny the feeling nature of the experience. By trying to approach the emotional experience from a logical perspective, one not only denies the feeling, one denies the function, and consequently, the complete, authentic emotional system contained within all human bodies. Recalling the great expectations of computers as they came into people's lives forty or so years ago, people speculated about serving robots that were more human-like because they could be programmed with emotions. With curriculum such as "anger management", one can speculate about humans who have been trained to be more robotic, functioning on pure logic. As for now, before major human adaptation occurs, one may be able to mask the feeling by replacing it with rationalization, but inevitably unresolved emotions will seek release. Put enough of these bottled up, repressed emotions together and eventually the person is going to erupt like a volcano or a gun-totting child. Drugs can be used, are being used, but unavoidably the emotional response will have to be recognized and resolved.

I do believe the children are trying to please grown-ups, to work with adults, because they do love and look to grown-ups for answers and guidance. I also believe that as adults and parents, people want the best for the children. Yet, the creative potential is potent, and the inner drive is there to propel each person to the optimum fulfillment of his or her unique life mission. Somehow the structure of society seems at odds with this potential and drive. Adults have grown into an acceptance of the repression of the creative energy. They have often traded their beloved dreams of what could be for the acquisition of money (insurance for the future) and the comforts of technology.

The children are not there yet, and, in some cases, they are rebelling against the adult way of doing things. This is not out of a lack of love. Actually, it is done in the name of love, a love of who they really are, creative beings capable of miraculous acts. Through bizarre behavior and resistance to the establishment, many children ask adults to reevaluate what modern, western society stands for and to find a way to accept and allow them to grow into the people they really are. Children have been doing this for centuries. It is the call of youth to question and explore cultural change. Somewhere along the way adult members of society have diverted their focus, lost faith in their inner knowing, and breathed life into a system that sets itself apart from the natural world and denies the spiritual aspect of being human.

The optimistic side of me says, "Great! If I can see and understand where I've gone astray, then I can go back and try something different. After all I'm chock full of amazing creative potential, and I've trusted my own inner knowing before. It has brought success. Surely, the wisdom of my own childhood experience, which is being reflected back to me from millions of young faces, can spiral me to ever greater heights."

I encourage you to think this through. Let us blend our creative potential. Together we can realize the excitement of adapting to the wondrous, natural world we live in and share. Beyond mere adaptation, we can add our authentic and unique song to the chorus of life and bring forth a time of renewal and rebirth.

# Chapter 4

# Expectations, Judgment, and Fear

Why have our voices become a weak cacophonous buzz?

It is not too many years after one is born that one becomes subject to expectations. Initially, they are there waiting in the wings, because at first a child does not realize that anything is required or expected of him or her. The newborn infant is totally oblivious to the message in the brand new soccer ball his or her father brought to the hospital or the information on college funds that came in the mail. For now, ignorance is bliss and to be is enough.

Remember the important lessons of play, remaining in the present moment and letting go of the end product? Expectations by their nature defy both: they are a product of linear thinking, comparisons. When there are expectations, a set of results has been anticipated. One believes specified results will occur in the future if prescribed actions are followed. As one knows in real life, as often as not, people are disappointed because their expectations are not met.

*Awakening Wisdom from Innocence*

As I write this I have been exceedingly frustrated because I expected to have all my remodeling done before the holidays. For five months I have lived with mess, dust, furniture, and boxes shoved in all the wrong places. Thanksgiving is just around the corner, and I can't seem to make a decision on how to redo the floors, the most extensive and expensive part of the remodeling job. My frustration and the pressure are directly related to expectations that are probably not going to be met. Since I have worked hard to fulfill the required obligations, I am beginning to feel cheated. I'm denying the balance and harmony of the natural world and trying to force my will on the little slice of life over which I have claimed dominion.

Having expectations is not necessarily a bad thing, but since one does not know what the future holds, it is beneficial and healthy to remain flexible. Surrounding my work with expectations, I have already decided on the final outcome of an action or series of actions, as in my own desire to have a remodeled house by the holidays. At this point, in my mind at least, nothing less will do. Anything short of meeting my goal is failure, and once again, I will judge myself as incompetent, financially disabled, and unrealistic. A nice gift before

*Dolores Calley*

Christmas, a wonderful mood to bring with me as my family arrives to celebrate the year's happiest of seasons. Instead of enjoying the people whom I love and am looking forward to seeing, I'll look around and reinforce my inability to complete projects and make my home beautiful. No one will be very good at bringing me out of it either. Instead, I'll waste our precious time robbing the focus of everyone's activities because my expectations have not been met! And at this point I am only dealing with how my house looks. What if John thinks Christmas needs a personally cut down tree and, to save time, I've already bought a pre-cut one? How about Michael? Maybe he is looking forward to the latest computer game, and they are sold out. And Wendel may be a vegetarian, and the extras I've cooked to go with the turkey don't really seem like a special Christmas dinner to him. This is a list that can go on and on and may well contain some conflicting expectations. Isn't my family setting themselves up for a lovely Christmas?

Having already determined the final results for the perfect picture of Christmas in my head, generally two major things happen for me personally. I set myself up for frustration and disappointment, and I am blind to an outcome that may work out better for me and everyone else in the long run. If I remember that nature seeks harmony in a bigger picture, the frustrating short term result often paves the way for a deeper, richer result in the future. Unfortunately, once I attach my feelings of success to a predetermined result, I am unlikely to recognize other possible scenarios. By neglecting the present I erroneously seek my picture of harmony or peace in some nebulous time in the future, and once I get to that future my focus will again miss the moment because I am too busy anticipating and making plans for the next future. Add to all this, my vision is limited to begin with. I am unable to see all the events that will come together as the future that will come to pass for me. Now isn't it silly to put so much emphasis on an illusion of being in control of my future?

But people seem to do this over and over, rarely realizing they have chosen to set themselves up for stress. Somehow individuals feel a greater sense of control by selecting an outcome ahead of time. The mere act of selecting gives a feeling of power over one's life, but all the missed marks certainly impact self-esteem and a sense of security in one's ability to control the way things work out. Along with this people are obviously not very good at predicting and fulfilling their future, and by continuing to try and force their will on the future, they are ignoring the lessons of the present. Not only do individuals do this to themselves, but they set each other up for the same experience of failure. Decisions about a partner's role, involvement with children or housework, and another's place in life, often diminish the growth of the relationship and the comfort of home. All anyone has to honestly do is let go of the expectations and experience each moment, however the moment presents itself.

Think of the roles people play, son, daughter, sister, brother, husband, wife, friend, doctor, secretary, and many, many more. Each of these roles come with certain expectations, not only the personal ones, but also all the expectations people on the other side of the role carry about one's behavior in fulfilling the role properly. Who can be the perfect sister or husband when it comes with some very conflicting expectations? Some of these expectations are totally trivial, but they are there, and someone may be breathing great importance into them. Aside from losing one's true self in trying to keep up with everyone else's expectations, more often than not, one just does not make the grade. Like a slow, steady drip all the advice and criticism erodes a sense of personal power and confidence. Remember, there was a time in most everyone's past when they lived in the moment and confidently stepped out into the world ready to freely explore.

Probably the role with the smallest pile of expectations is as the new parent. Oh, the in-laws may have lots of advice, and a new parent may squirm around under the microscope for a while, but that beautiful little baby, the initiator of new parenthood, will shortly be smiling, expecting only to be loved and to love. The baby will never notice the ineptness or remind his or her parents of a better way to fulfill his or her simple, basic needs. A baby doesn't carry expectations because he has not learned the technique yet. That is why when a parent provides care from a source of love; they will rarely do harm to their child.

Later, as the child has a chance to compare, the parent may become too fat, too dumb, too strict, and so on. These expectations come with the territory when one is in the forest of growing up. I believe that these expectations of cultural experience are learned behavior. Children learn them when they learn that humankind is in control on this planet. They are taught what outcomes are expected and what actions are required. These beliefs are handed over as a human right, the right to control all with which anyone makes contact. But, as a person controls, he or she also becomes subject to being controlled. Today, there is a lot of corruption and many special interest groups lobbying for power and laws to justify the rightness of their position. No doubt about it, this is control over how one may express his or her individual potential. And if one seeks control through expectations, there will be an outside world that seeks control with greater expectations. The individual gets lost in the demands of other people's perceptions. And instead of growing into the full authenticity of self, the individual learns to settle into a static profile of some nebulous average citizen.

In school, it doesn't take long for a child to realize that certain behavior and achievement are expected. The child is learning the role of a student. The behavior and accomplishment becomes the measure of who the child is, and every person who has attended public school has been conditioned in this manner. Young people are judged on

*Awakening Wisdom from Innocence*

these very limited aspects time and again. Eventually, they begin to identify and accept themselves as Suzy the "A" student or Jimmy, the "discipline problem." Once that identity is taken, the child has found his or her place in the world that extends beyond the family. He knows who he is, and she just has to perform the role properly. The goal becomes conformity and the expression of potential must yield to the social framework. If the experience is uncomfortable, the authentic child is whisked away into a dark closet (somewhere close to the heart) where he or she will be protected and safe. The true being has no place in a society where his or her expression is repressed. Rebirthing and awakening the inner child are present day hints that suggest a deep, inner understanding of this and a desire to reconnect with the authentic self.

Maybe the road to hell is paved with bad expectations. These expectations come from an apparent consensus of, often well documented, judgments on how these roles are to be properly played out. There are volumes of laws to attest to the fact. Unfortunately, the public school system, one of the earliest formal training centers, serves as a good example of this. By second or third grade, sometimes earlier, most children have been assessed by the teachers and school officials. Often it is a very casual assessment, but it is usually carried on the "permanent record" of the student. Mary is very creative; Billy is hyperactive; Jane's a slow student; Alan is gifted in math. Before the school year starts, the new teacher usually has either directly or subtly established some expectations for many students. Most everyone knows the classic example of being pegged a "C" student in the beginning of the term and being unable to do any better than a "C" in that class. Sometimes the student's work can improve during the course of the semester, but the teacher's expectations may be much more difficult to adjust. And that rigid form of judgment is often a tactic of the parents and friends as well. In society people are quick to label people. A financial benefit often accompanies the label. Teachers, parents, and friends often miss that which is wonderful in the child and stifle the child's unique, talented personhood. Personally, I would welcome the light of authenticity in each person I meet. I would like to share the individuality, join with it, and beam the ray of humanity as brilliantly as the sun that is celebrated for just rising and bringing forth another day. My friend,

*Awakening Wisdom from Innocence*

who practices homeopathy, once told me that being present and participating is enough. Being present seems to be an important feature and, if one has tucked away the real self, being present is difficult. Americans, in particular, are always preparing or worrying about the future. They rarely stop to enjoy just being, except as in a frenetic, consumerist vacation.

No one has to pigeonhole himself or herself or any one else. Whether it is a habit or not, people choose to do it. The choice is made because faith in one another and oneself has been worn down by expectations and the judgments that have attached to them like leeches. Today, in society, in most situations, someone is held responsible. There are no accidents, no meaningful lessons from being on the wrong side of an event. I know that I have had some very valuable insights from going through the rough part of a life drama. Though I may not want to repeat the experience, I certainly have no regrets about my participation. The dramas help me discover who I am. Instead of facing this type of adversity with acceptance and appreciation, many people become the "poor victim" and look for an opportunity to get rich or make "the creeps" pay. Either is an unhealthy focus that blinds the person to the gift of living through and overcoming the difficulty.

The blindness comes in the form of judgment, and when one starts to look at the volumes of law, the quantity of special interest groups, and the corporate and club regulations, one realizes that developing the "right way" for re-made, role-fulfilling people to conduct their lives has become a matter of big business and everyone else's policing role. Frankly, it is terribly restricting, especially to an infusion of new and creative ideas. It is alien to the core of being human. Remember the spiral of potential? Each person has his or her set of talents based upon his or her unique exploration and learning. This personal experience must also include the difficult lesson, so that evolution takes place.

Visit a book store and see all the "how to" and self-help books. Notice how many of the author's come with qualifications, letters after their names, and degrees from institutes of higher learning. These people are often presenting their personal opinions on the right way to conduct a specific aspect of life. Many people allow someone else to take responsibility and specify which path is right for them.

This is done by denying faith and security in one's self and refusing to think through what is valuable to experience personally. Often, one gives away the power in his or her life to someone who has not experienced as much.

Part of the routine of having a child today is to go to classes, read books on the subject, and watch a birthing video. People seem to think it's not going to come to completion unless they have learned about the process. Educated or not, once the fetus is in the womb, the experience will be. When my "high risk" pregnancy came to the moment of birth, I really had a crowd. It was one of those "lights, camera, action" moments, and I was center stage. Thank God I wasn't sleeping. Since I was the star, I asked each of the ten to twelve attendees to introduce themselves and tell me what their job was. As the knife was poised for the first cut, I said, "Can you imagine, some women just go off into the woods to give birth?" Once too many experts decide on the appropriate way to do something, simplicity can go right out the door. Each person needs to remember that there are many valid methods for each task.

*Dolores Calley*

Once Michael was pulled from my body, I heard the hushed exclamations, "He's healthy! I can't believe it, he's fine." And the chorus of "he's healthy" continued for the next twenty-four hours. I can hardly imagine what they were all expecting. Many months earlier I had left Michael in God's capable hands, and just loved him. There was no doubt in my mind that he would be anything but perfect, no matter how the perfect came to me.

The expectations, heavy with judgments, need to be replaced with desire steeped in love, the unconditional kind. By expressing love-laced desire and allowing the universe to bring it forth in the optimum (based on balance and harmony) manner, individuals permit eyes that see a much bigger picture of life to set the web of circumstance in place. What comes to pass inevitably works best in the life of the individual. Often, when a person has come through a difficult time, they look back and appreciate the long-term result because the outcome was more effective than what they thought would work. By the simple act of recognizing one's authentic desire, expressing it to all there is, and releasing the expected outcome, one reaffirms faith in the ever-present beacon of harmony.

*Awakening Wisdom from Innocence*

The following is a practice of mine, and it is effective. Go outside and request something from deep within your heart and then let it go. Know that it will come to pass, maybe not quite the way you anticipate. Allow your senses to heighten and your limitations to expand. Let the gift come in it's own time and manner.

Why have people turned these desires into expectations? People feel more secure with the completed picture that an expectation allows. Human beings like to think, and when they do, they are compelled to use a two-point (past and future) system. If one looks at the past, one sees that an acceptable way to settle a dispute is by force or the threat of force. On a worldwide scale, much of the threat of force comes from thinking up and creating more powerful weapons of destruction. As scientists create bombs that can be dropped, people distance themselves from the site of destruction. No one has to "get in there" and taste the blood and listen to the cries. This allows a real justification of force because the goal of winning can be achieved without pain or direct contact with the enemy. Since people do not directly realize the ramifications by physical, hands-on presence at the scene, the win can be celebrated and the devastation viewed in comfort on TV. That way the real and the imaginary can be interchanged as one's comfort level dictates. Once again the emotional make-up can be denied the feeling expression. The cycle feeds itself, forcing a win-lose situation where the one with the greatest force wins and calls the shots. Each time a win occurs, the victory reinforces power and force as the appropriate avenue to bring forth the expectation based on the judgment that winning is better.

Modern society has become comfortable with this system, but if one looks at the children, one can often see different systems, more humane ways of dealing with conflicts and working with one another. Last year, Michael and his friends developed various clubs, the bouncy ball club, song club, cartoon club, video game club, and others. Their casual hierarchy really impressed me, especially since it was completely based on second grade justice and fairness.

Whoever thought up the club focus became the first captain, and chose a second and third captain. The captains' authority included selecting the activities of the club and deciding on who could join. If the captains did a good job, the first captain could become an advanced captain and the second and third would then move up the ranks. If the captains did something the group felt wasn't fair or correct, they got bumped down the ranks. If they straightened up they could regain the responsibility and authority of the captain position again by moving up the ranks. Advanced captains were the only ones who had second chances. If one were just a member and did something that was looked upon badly by the rest of the group, the captains temporarily threw that member out of the club. If a member did not like the way the club was going, they could start their own club. Even today the model is still there, whoever has the idea becomes first captain. The structure is simple, flexible, and easy for the average child to access. Each participant has opportunity to lead or to follow, and participation is based on free will. Creativity and new clubs are encouraged by the very nature of the hierarchy. Once a person decides to join, they have to conform a little, but there is no obligation and no force. The clubs remain strong after one and a half years. New ones are added regularly.

One thing that has put a bit of a damper on the clubs is a threat to tell the teacher when a captain bumps someone temporarily. The teacher has power and can force things, making life basically unpleasant. Since the teacher is an adult, he or she has grown up with force as a predominant means of resolving conflict, and in the playground, the teacher is law. Although this is an example of a mild fear, it brings up the missing element in the win lose scenario—fear.

Individuals within modern western society spend an amazing amount of time feeding their fears, working to protect themselves from their fears, and blaming other things and people for THEIR fear. When John was a wee baby, a young man climbed three flights of fire escape stairs at my apartment building. While I was taking a shower, he came through my kitchen window. Since John was only a few months old, I had left the bathroom door open so I would hear him if he cried. The shadow of the stranger moved on and off the white door of the bathroom as the fellow moved about my kitchen. I knew a stranger was in my house, not far from my baby's room. I had time to sort through my feelings and consciously chose a course of action.

Even under the stress it was an interesting experience because there were a lot of intense and rapidly changing emotions affecting my thinking. Initially, I thought that I could ignore him, and he would go away. As that thought was finishing, a second and third

*Awakening Wisdom from Innocence*

followed like the waves of contractions near the end of labor. Next, I looked around for a weapon with which to protect my baby and myself. That thought dissipated in the realization that my best possibilities were a toilet bowl brush and a plastic shampoo bottle. All this occurred in a matter of seconds.

The finale exploded in a crescendo of anger that moved through my body like the urge to push during childbirth. Starting in my very toes, cell after cell of my body was alerted, and the command of "charge" took over. I was mad! Shampoo bubbles dripped onto my naked shoulders as I grabbed a towel. Leaving the shower on to maintain the element of surprise, I ran into the kitchen spitting angry words like rapid-fire ammunition. I was highly alert and well prepared to drop my towel and squish out his eyeballs and bite through his jugular vein if necessary. The reaction came from an overwhelming concern for my baby's safety.

I could feel the perpetrator's terror as he stumbled over the windowsill in his rush to run away from me. Once he was gone I reviewed the image of him tumbling out the window, never taking his eyes off me. With slow, objective precision I organized the details of his face and physique and then dialed 911.

That little life drama hinted at an amazing potential of personal power and strength. I had no weapon, heck, I didn't even have clothes on, and yet somehow I, the supposed victim, totally turned the tables and left the invader scared and quivering. Without a doubt I had experienced a very primal strength that held communion with Indian mothers, wolf mothers, bear mothers, and caveman mothers. There was absolutely no fear, just rage, a rage that pushed all other emotions aside. Can you imagine being that filled with love?

I learned that within each mother (probably fathers too) there is a protective power that far surpasses any insurance policy, weapon, or alarm system that can be purchased. This inner power is always with the individual. When a person is guided by it, the experience is awesome. From that day forward, I have felt capable of protecting myself and my children, except for a year or two when John and Wendel were quite young, and I succumbed to fear.

At that time I was divorcing their father and leaving the state. I had two incidents when someone was trying to break into my house while I was home. Each time I could hear the stranger at the window or door. Once I even saw a lock of hair hanging peacefully between the crack in my curtains. It was somewhat terrifying, but I was still fortified with the memory of my initial encounter with an invader. With the help of my Mother's lovable but protective Weimaraner and the police, John, Wendel, and I safely remained at home until we could board a plane and start a new life.

A feeling of safety was with me until a second series of incidents in our new home. Someone would ring my doorbell, and when I went to the door, no one was there. It was at this point I began to break down. I allowed all these experiences to come together and grow into one major fear. Since my ex-husband called on a rather regular basis threatening my life and the safety of my little ones, the fear was fed regularly. For a good year and a half, I slept very little. My mind was filled with deadly encounters, mutilations, missing babies, and utter devastation in my life.

At last, the day came when I looked back at the over-a-year of terror. Every horrible thing I could think of had happened, but it had only happened in my mind. I was the one scaring myself. Finally, I could view it as an illusion, very powerful, crippling, and very SELF-DIRECTED. Once I understood this, I also realized that I did not have to be afraid anymore. The choice was always mine. Through it all I had chosen to be fearful, and I had done what I needed to do to keep that fear at the forefront of my life. I thought fearful thoughts constantly, and I believed that scary things would happen.

This was another of those "hallmark" moments. My picture of life was, and continues to be, based upon where I direct the viewfinder of my camera. I can focus on a dead, scary, and deteriorating picture of life, or I can set my sites on the stimulating, vibrant, and ever changing vistas. Even if the cultural message on TV is one of death and violence, the individual can redirect his or her sight and change the view. Anyone can choose an optimistic view, and nourish it daily with peaceful, happy, and secure images.

Look at society's vision of life; watch the nightly news; check out what is on TV. The media feeds people a major dose of fear. Children are encouraged to swim in the murky waters of scare every day. I believe that feeding fear is a major priority in modern culture. Just look at the different kinds of insurances available, the

*Awakening Wisdom from Innocence*

proliferation of protection service companies, and the on-going news coverage of heinous crimes. The quantity of examples I could mention is astronomical. Major decisions regarding our country and our interactions with each other are based primarily on the same illusion of fear that I finally had to face for my own sanity and well-being.

One difference between my personal fear and society's fear is that, at least, I manipulated my own fear. The individual members of society are allowing themselves to be manipulated by outside sources. The great danger in this situation is that society makes important decisions bashed upon what scares them. Such a society can be easily controlled. They are asking for manipulation because they feel so insecure. If, on a personal level, individuals overcome their fear, the society will be free, strong, and unlikely to be directed through manipulation.

Consider the average child between the ages of one and three. Most of them are fearless. It is the high time for drowning in the backyard pool, suffocation in a plastic bag, and poisoning from any number of dangerous cleaning substances. (Please notice that the dangers above are not of the natural world. Man, for adult convenience) has developed them all. Even with the hurdles put in place by his or her parents, most of the toddlers do go on to grow up, but something happens as they move into young childhood. They begin developing fears. How could they not? Already they have probably been subject to the visual effects of well over 100 deaths on TV. "No" and "be careful" have undoubtedly filtered through their ears on a daily basis, and I'll bet, the "don't talk to strangers" conversation has taken place. And, this fear awareness will get reinforced and intensified as the sweet little one enters school and participates more maturely with the adult world. What has grown along with the toddler is the awareness of danger. The same dangers have been there since the baby's birth, but, his or her little viewfinder has been skillfully and continually brought to focus on potentially scary things and situations. This is done because the adults are afraid. The adults pass the fear on as a big part of the focus of modern society.

*Awakening Wisdom from Innocence*

One very cold and wintry afternoon, I hear a mournful wail coming from somewhere outside, "I'm gonna die. On, I'm gonna die. Help," the little voice beseeched.

I grabbed my coat and was stuffing an arm into the sleeve as I opened the front door. Across the street was the young neighbor boy. I rushed to him, bent down to his level, hugged him, and said, "Jarrett, what's wrong, honey?"

All that was audible was a wet sob coming from deep within his small body. So I took his hand and led him across to my kitchen, complete with freshly baked cookies. As I warmed milk for a cup of hot chocolate, I again asked Jarrett what had upset him so.

He was afraid. The school bus had dropped him off after kindergarten, and when he arrived at his door, no one was home. He knew that he was little, so he figured he was going to die. The irony of this incident is that his aunt, whom he dearly loved, lived only two doors down from him on the same side of the street. Since he was so paralyzed by the fearful weight of finding himself alone, Jarrett could neither remember his mother's instructions, nor think how easy it would be to walk to his aunt's house, something he often did.

*Dolores Calley*

One might wonder how often, out of simple fear-based thinking, adults are unable to think something through or move in a sensible direction. Once a manipulator or power hungry individual is thrown into the mix, trouble is not far away. Through the act of giving up personal power to fear, one leaves a hole that can easily be filled by someone or something that does not have the victim's best interest at heart. If one can overcome the fear, strength and power are theirs. I have experienced this. To encourage a feeling of safety, one needs to give up activities that feed fear and, instead, do things that empower.

People do not need to set themselves up to become a victim of anything. It is ironic that often the best way to become a victim is to do all the "right things" to avoid being a victim. Some will continue to be the victim until they choose to shatter the illusion of protection they believe comes from outside them. As with many good things, the safety and security comes from within. Until individuals understand this, they may face dramas that will help them uncover this truth. Paradoxically, the fear of death seems to lead to a fear of living.

*Awakening Wisdom from Innocence*

Once I could see the fear illusion I had created with my mind, I had to take time and measures to untangle myself from the web of fear I had wrapped around myself. First, I looked at fear as being the fear of death. And in the instance with Wendel's suicide attempts and John and the man who broke into my apartment, indeed, physical death could have been the result. If I believed in some type of afterlife in heaven, why would I be worried about my or my children's death? If I believed in being recycled into the earth and becoming a part of nature, then I would not remember any of this life on earth, so why fear death? In all of this thinking, I knew one thing for certain—MY CHILDREN AND I WERE GONING TO DIE. If my death was inevitable, it was pretty dumb to fear death and not, in some way, address the fear. Acceptance would be a much better place to be. Maybe I could even move beyond acceptance to gratitude and anticipation. These two latter ideas, at times, seem even more ideal.

Since I often see the truths of the universe reflected again and again in people's lives and the world, this is what I came up with. What if there is a God, and he built us a playground (the earth) the same as parents might build their children a fort or jungle gym. And then God said, "My dear children go out and play," as any parent might say, "all of you outside and play." Maybe God is the father of humanity in spirit so he knows those on earth cannot kill themselves or permanently harm each other no matter what they do. Thus, he lets them play any game they like. He knows that physical death is the vehicle used to return home. People may have killed each other in a game of war or suffered fatal injuries when their car crashed, but when it is over, they take with them only the insight they have gained from the play as they return home.

I do not know if God has created earth as a playground, but this belief appeals to me. Not only does it satisfy my linear thinking and suggest reasons for some of life's cruelties, it has helped me release a lot of fear. Children are sometimes hurt during their play, but since God has to be so much bigger, well beyond my ability to comprehend, I might also be bigger, working to uncover an ever-expanding picture of myself. And just maybe, the source of who and what I am is eternal and truly untouchable to the cruel and dangerous aspects of life on earth.

# Chapter 5

# Diversity, Unity, and Acceptance

Instead of wallowing like pigs in the mud of expectations, judgment, and fear, maybe humanity should adopt a new picture, a garden from which people can begin to live life in greater harmony. Using the picture of earth as a playground allows society to choose with awareness the game to be played. The big problem with choice is there are so many people, and communication is not always easy. Add to that the many different perspectives to incorporate, some of which appear to be conflicting. I use the word appear because the conflict is present due to the lens filtering the ideas. Many of the ideas are perfectly acceptable. The lens is clouded with judgments and held in place by the rigidity of the way people generally think. Along with linear thinking, which carries the two points of past and present, critical thinking is used. Again, it's a two point system, which assesses correct or incorrect, right or wrong, or good or bad depending on the data presented. In evaluating the information, the conclusion is most often judgmental. Just look at the term, "critical" thinking. Oh, people try and convince themselves that the thinking is all very objective by only recognizing numbers, measurable parameters, reproducible occurrences, and facts, but one can only go so far with human abilities to observe accurately. There is also a limit to the capability of instrumentation. Hence, the evaluation that comes as a product of critical thinking or objective reasoning may be incomplete, depicting only one plane of a multifaceted gem. Someone grabs onto one little piece of the puzzle and goes off half-cocked celebrating the amazing discovery of a new and completed puzzle. This discovery then becomes the foundation for further studies and the basis for conclusions that may follow. Unfortunately, sometimes the foundation idea is faulty. For a long time scientists made conclusions about how the universe worked based on the model of a flat earth sitting in the middle of the cosmos.

By understanding the process of thinking, a person can begin to see how this process directs and impacts all aspects of living. Presently, linear or bipolar (two opposing points) ways of thinking separate information into little individual facts or conclusions.

Someone is either for or against, black or white, a winner or a loser. In the two-point thinking systems, new information is compared to previous knowledge and then categorized. If the new information does not quite fit, it is categorized with the most similar data. This filing system restricts the choices, limits proper evaluation of the information that crosses over into other categories, becomes unwieldy to work with, and increases the occurrence of error. Conclusions may have been reached based on comparison to improperly categorized information that formed the foundation for the new conclusion. A thought that is genuinely new and relative to nothing in the present belief system has no place to reside. It is either trashed, ridiculed or a "temptation from the devil."

I really "think" people need to incorporate a new system, not to replace the old one, but to use as another flexible and expanded technique for processing information. Perhaps then there will be a method that will allow people to take all those little puzzle pieces humanity has been collecting, thinking they were whole and complete, and incorporate them into a much larger and more valid picture. This system also needs to allow for variables and unknowns.

*Dolores Calley*

This system has to recognize the possibility that the basis for comparison may be erroneous and that there may be energies beyond our present sensory scope or technological capabilities that influence results.

This new technique needs to allow information to flow freely and be available like all the bits on the Internet. The new thought process could be like a wonderful Sunday brunch buffet. Anyone could fill up their plate with all different kinds of ideas, absorb them, blend the various flavors, take a taste instead of wasting a whole portion, try new items and combinations, and be grateful for the continuing supply of fresh dishes. The buffet is a very flexible way to serve, satisfying many individual palates, allowing free choice, and encouraging the exploration of new and exotic dishes. When food is served as critical thinking, it is categorized as breakfast, lunch, or dinner, or sorted as to appetizer, main course, and dessert. Combinations are decided, joined together as a meal, and served in the same or similar ways over and over again. Think about which type of eating experience you prefer and get a glimpse of your comfortable mode of thinking.

Comfortable is nice, but any one of us can take the risk, tap into human potential, and find ways to view the same thing or situation from myriad of angles and focuses. (Maybe that is why there are so many of us.) But, this is unlikely to happen when using a two-point thinking system. There needs to be a way to incorporate more points and whole other systems, even those of which no one is presently aware. If judgment, assessment, and categorizing are withheld, the mental void can be filled with possibilities and evolving relationships. Maybe working together human beings can find a more satisfying and human way of structuring our society. Who knows, society might even muster up the courage to let the children, in their innocence, lead the way.

The very first thing that needs to begin to diminish is judgment. No more good, bad, black, or white. Instead, there should be a validation of existence and the right to be. Once the idea is given recognition for it's right to exist, each person can choose to accept the idea and incorporate it into his or her thinking, or to leave it floating for the present. Who knows, years from now that same idea may become a comforting thought in my heart or a glaring reality in my life.  Denying the idea's existence only makes the idea harder to find if I need to revisit it or more difficult to accept when I am faced with it's reality.  And the thought does no harm by being because I have the right and power to decide where the thought belongs in my life, and I am not afraid of the idea.  Allowing the existence of this pool of ideas will encourage people to stop judging and trying to control what others should think.  An extensive idea bank will encourage individuals to explore the fruits of their own minds because of the challenging abundance of thought.

One can follow information processing by using the existence of the devil as the embodiment of evil as an example.  Hanging out in space is the idea that evil is real and present on the earth in the form of the devil.  Sitting in a Sunday school class many years ago, little Dee Dee is first introduced to the idea that the devil exists.  The teacher sucks up the thought and, being a good two-point thinker, she spews the idea over the class like a fearful, fast moving fire.  She stresses the fact that there is no doubt that the devil exists, and he is mean, bad to the core.  His mission is to take over people's hearts.  The idea makes it's way into the mind of innocent, trusting little Dee

*Awakening Wisdom from Innocence*

Dee. The little girl looks the thought over, says, "okay", and then remembers that God takes care of her. She feels safe so she puts the idea aside.

As childhood continues there are other times when the devil's name comes up, and the association is always with evil and fear. Dee Dee grows up and marries an alcoholic. They have a baby. When there is no money for food, there is money for beer. Dee Dee thinks of the devil. When the dog's head is split open and people are hurt, Dee Dee wants to kill the devil that lives in the house. That anger, the emotion that the devil elicits, is not due to the proven existence of the devil. It is due to the judgment that follows the idea around. The reality of an evil person comes as the judgment which was wed to the thought by the Sunday school teacher long ago. Dee Dee gave up her authentic feelings, whatever they may have been, because the appropriate emotional response was vividly displayed at the time the idea of the devil was introduced. The emotion can no longer be separated from the idea of the existence of the devil.

The baby that Dee Dee and her husband had grows up. The son is the joy and happiness of his mother's life. The son asks, "Mom, tell me about my father."

Dee Dee cannot bring herself to say, "Your father is the devil. You are the son of the devil." She cannot say this because the son is good. How can this good son also be the son of the devil? In the two-point system there is good or bad, not both. So the opportunity is given for Dee Dee to begin to formulate her individual belief about the existence of the devil based upon her unique experience. How differently this marriage drama may have played out had Dee Dee been encouraged to come to her own, authentic conclusions about the existence of the devil. Now, she may need to go beyond the comfortable two-part method because the son has brought the idea beyond two points.

To Dee Dee, at this point, the puzzle of meanness and cruelty, all wrapped up in the idea of a devil within a man, seems limited and no longer able to supply a complete answer for the meanness and cruelty she has experienced. Now she must decide if the initial idea, encased in judgment, is a complete and valuable assessment of evil.

*Awakening Wisdom from Innocence*

If Dee Dee withholds judgment, because she has realized that maybe she is only seeing part of the elephant's neck instead of the whole animal, the alcoholic would not be categorized as mean or equated with the devil. The son would not be judged on the basis of the father because each would stand as an individual with ownership of his own behavior. Even if Dee Dee recognized and filed cruel acts as something to be avoided, a new way of thinking allows possibilities and relationships. Instead of going over the prepackaged idea complete with appropriate response, Dee Dee will have to use her brain and emotions to feed her evolving belief about evil. The new focus would allow Dee Dee to explore other options in response to the father's damaging behavior. She might ask, "why am I in this drama? What do I need to learn? Would I do it again for the presence of the wonderful son in my life? Has the alcoholic man given me a gift in the son and in awareness of my own personal power? Does the alcoholic drink to destroy the family?"

Today each of us is bombarded with political correctness and diversity training. The ideas may be based on a desire to interact with greater kindness and cooperation, but if this interaction is done superficially and judgmentally, it comes off as a joke. It also serves to cause greater separation and deterioration of human relationships. In such a situation, true individual emotions are denied expression. In their place are judgments and responses that comply with some established norm. This norm invites people to give up their individuality to a robotic sameness in order to maintain an established social structure. It also requires one to give up thinking his or her own authentic thoughts, humanity's great gift to the earth, and merely mimic the spoon fed tenets and standards that seem to be formulated by others in a wasteland devoid of humanness.

I can recall a time in my youth when computers were beginning to take hold. As scientists discussed the potential uses of computer chip technology, they spoke of developing robots to do some of the menial tasks in the home. They even pictured a day when robots would be more human-like. This could happen if scientists could incorporate feelings into the robot's programming. People believed this was possible and that the direction of development would move toward making robots more like familiar friends.

*Awakening Wisdom from Innocence*

Looking at where this technology has led, I think man has done the exact opposite. Delighting in computer creations, scientists are finding ways to make people more robot-like. Computer chips, which are now easily attached to or implanted in the human body, are available for a wide variety or tasks, including monitoring glucose levels, sending messages to non-functioning limbs, tracking missing people, and even deducting funds from bank accounts. I have little doubt that there are other tasks, some insidious, some beneficial, that implanted chips can do. Along with the ability to make human beings more machine-like, society is intellectualizing human emotions, both how to respond and what to repress. Society is playing designer genetics with future generations and developing all sorts of replacement parts to mold the perfect physical image. As the image is polished and cared for, the foundation is showing the results of such long-term neglect. Many people do not realize it, but this desire and demand for man-made perfection spells the end to the individual and a big hello to Star Trek's Borg (sameness).

As species on our planet regularly disappear, often due to man's desire for space, food, and power, the wonderful diversity earth has displayed diminishes. As species become extinct, scientists are becoming aware of the delicate balance that shifts, sways and suffers with the loss. Perhaps the final lesson is to participate as non-thinking, non-feeling units devoted totally to satisfying the whims of some outside force. If society continues to ignore potential, deny responsibility for actions, demand conformity, and cripple thinking processes, humans are preparing for the lesson that would allow everyone to see what real sameness is truly about. This certainly gives cause to consider expanding human thinking techniques and withholding judgment. Sameness is a far cry from unity.

Unity only works when strong individuals are consciously and cooperatively participating under the umbrella of a common vision. The strength of the unified group is in their diversity because the differentiation allows an abundance of potential, quick response to myriad of possible changes in the environment, and a loving support system for all. The successful group, united under a common goal that is supported by love, has an open, honest communication that includes all members equally.

A most perfect model of a diversified, unified system can be found in our bodies. Even within the separate body organ systems, such as the heart, lung, digestive, and so on, there is individualization. Each moment trillions of unique cells are interacting independently and cooperatively to the ever-changing environment they share. The undisputed goal of harmony and balance is achieved through the many and varied functions that individualization supports and encourages. All the unique actions of which our bodies are capable would not be possible except for the trillions of cells that fulfill their authentic and unique purpose with awareness and obvious love.

If one day brain cells decided that they were the most important cells in the body and if those brain cells decided that all the other cells were placed in the body to serve the brain, think of what chaos would occur within the body. Instead of working together to maintain harmony and balance, organ systems would have to reorganize, develop guard cells to protect territory, deal with fear of attack, build weapons, become mistrustful, compete, and basically go on living with a sense of fear and isolation. For example, the function of digesting food would be diluted with the need to protect, the anxiety of being separated from the rest of the being, the insecurity of dwindling love and support, and the need to justify existence. The function of digestion, the purpose of each cell within the digestive system, would no longer be performed in the fullness of love and the focus of harmony.

The generations that follow would slowly loose the understanding of their purpose because the big brain cells would have forced a major change. And this major change would be in belief only. The rest of the changes would come from supporting the idea that brain cells are the important ones. Whether or not brain cells were more important would not be the issue. The fact that other cells bought into the idea would carry all the meaning. This support in the belief is what sets up the change in the reality. From the time that the idea of unity is replaced with the belief that brain cells reign, the reality of the body takes on a different path, one which alters, rather dramatically, the original purpose of working together in an atmosphere of equality. This new reality is also an illusion of the original nature of all the individual cells involved.

*Awakening Wisdom from Innocence*

The illusion strengthens with each new generation. As each new generation comes into existence, they slowly move further and further away from the original purpose of digesting food for the benefit of the whole organism. Of course, their ability to process food would wait as a potential that could at any time expand to a much higher expression. The growing illusion would set their new purpose as serving the brain cells through the process of digestion. The brain cells' requirements may not meet the needs of others within the system. Eventually, as the brain cells subjugate more and more individual cells and organ systems, aligning their purposes to the new reality, cell systems would change. Instead of working to benefit the whole being, understanding that what benefits the whole works in the best interest of all the individual cells, now everyone would be altering their needs to the desires of only one part of the organism, the brain. Some organ systems could disappear altogether, submitting to extinction because there is no longer purpose or place for their existence. Other systems may decide to deny their uniqueness and emulate brain cells in order to survive. The original, fine-tuned, balanced, beautiful organism would cease to exist as it had in earlier times. The body would have become crippled by the shift in focus and purpose. The end of such a downward spiral could well result in the death of all. Or a new organism could develop, "the big brain". Of course, the continued existence of the "big brain" would rely on conquering and enslaving. Certainly, there are lessons in both bodies and their organizations.

In this analogy, one can go a step further. One can change the human body to the planet earth. If humanity is substituted for brain cells in the above example, one can see how setting the species apart from the natural world on earth and forgetting their place in the unity of life on the planet could cause a shift that would ripple down to the very microscopic organisms who call the same water and soil their home. Yet, the reaction from the animal and plant life has not been as illustrated above. Only the people have resorted to a response based on fear. The species other than human have merely adapted or disappeared from the planet. I believe this reaction serves to remind people that other views of reality are present on earth. No matter how competitive one life form becomes, others can respond with love. Perhaps the lesson in this response is one's duty to self and the

*Awakening Wisdom from Innocence*

individual example one brings forth within the universe. Maybe a reaction based on love serves to anchor on earth the potential each individual carries within his or her own personhood.

The idea of acceptance seems to be floating around in the buzzwords of "cultural diversity" and "political correctness". Unfortunately, this idea comes with an intellectualized set of rules (attend a sensitivity training class), and in this world that generally means some are accepted, but only by rejecting or undermining others. Judgment and linear thinking encourage rating and comparison. If one looks to the innocence of the very young, there is a wealth of true acceptance training.

Little moments with each of my children carry memories of a child's acceptance of others with no judgment of who the people were. Wendel had a conversation with a man at the grocery check out counter. The man was clearly drunk, and Wendel laughed and chatted away as if they were old friends. Other people were purposely avoiding the old fellow and whispering comments to each other. There were many moments with John in New York City. He could hardly pass up a blind, dirty, or otherwise obviously suffering

*Dolores Calley*

homeless person without dropping some change in their cup and sharing a few words. Michael, since he could walk, would enter a room and zero in on the person who sat alone, isolated. He never left without exchanging smiles and words with the lonely ones. Children do not read the signs that stand like road maps indicating the individuals who are to be avoided by their peers. Instead, the little ones follow the wisdom of their hearts.

Superficial acceptance, the illusion of acceptance deals with aspects of skin color and cultural celebrations. The real, deep acceptance comes from accepting another's beliefs and allowing that person the right of free expression of those beliefs. Allowing free expression does not require tossing one's own opinions and preferences into the wind and soaking up everyone else's beliefs. A person can be honest and true to individual beliefs while honoring another's ideas and beliefs. By validating another's right to believe as their heart dictates, a person reaffirms everyone's right to believe the truth of their heart's perspective.

America was based on people's desire for free expression of their beliefs. As with thoughts, nothing is given away by allowing differing beliefs to mingle with one's own beliefs. When a person or group of people set out to ostracize or destroy another because of differing perspectives, the attack only speaks of fear. This fear indicates that the beliefs of the destroyer sit atop active fault lines, and by exposing themselves to the beliefs of others, the earthquakes may begin. Perhaps the fearful person worries they will be left with nothing. But one is never left with a lack of beliefs. What often happens is the development of conflict between the judgment-laden thoughts and the emotionally directed beliefs. The way to strengthen beliefs is to bring alignment to the heart and the beliefs and then, put them out there through conversation and living experience; test them. If the belief does not withstand the test, the indication is for reevaluation of the belief. Since everyone has the power of choice, one can exercise that right and adjust the belief. No one needs to be a sheep blindly following the flock.

By participating in opportunities that test beliefs, one can begin to sort them out, to refine and formulate their own appropriate code of living. If a person wants to live in a world of real people, each person needs to allow others the same luxury. Volumes of laws, especially those dealing with personal choices, do not lend themselves to the right and responsibility of the authentic determination of individual beliefs. Ironically, the passing of laws has never stopped nor prevented the behavior for which it was written. These dictates also stifle each person's discovery of who they really are. There is sadness in the loss because the results support poor communication, lack of direction, and interaction based on mistrust. People, on an individual basis, are lost to themselves as well as society. Who knows, the day may come when each of us can project a hologram of who we think the world wants us to be.

Sharing beliefs with people who have had very different life experiences can allow one to see life in its very varied forms. This experience often enriches each of the participant's lives in a way beyond the experience available by either person alone. A beautiful little illustration of this is the deep impact Ruth, Michael's black mother, had on my life as well as Michael's.

Ruth, who was a casual friend during my pregnancy, offered to watch Michael prior to his birth. Ruth had arrived in America some years earlier as the bride of a Peace Corps volunteer. Prior to her

*Awakening Wisdom from Innocence*

wedding Ruth lived as a tribeswoman in Africa. Certainly, her life experience had been vastly different from mine. Amazingly, we had met when I felt I needed to find a very special baby-sitter for the child I was carrying. Ruth had two delightful little girls of her own, so when she said that she would like to care for Michael, I said yes. Three months after Michael came into the world, Ruth became his other mother.

Ruth was working on English literacy. Although she was not well educated by American standards, her knowledge of child rearing was exciting and new to me. In the morning when I dropped Michael off, Ruth would bend from the waist and, using a wide woven scarf, she would position Michael on her back and tie him in place. As the washing, hanging, vacuuming, and scrubbing was completed, Michael would peacefully rock and sway on Ruth's back. For Michael this daily contact with a beating heart and a warm, loving body must have been comforting and secure. I'm sure she chatted away to this baby because every time she changed a diaper, fed him, or otherwise attended to his needs, Ruth always asked permission form this tiny, non-verbal boy.

By this simple act of requesting, Ruth honored Michael as an individual complete with preferences and rights of choice. She never viewed him as an empty vessel waiting to be filled with the dictates and customs of his new society. I'm sure that Ruth had her understanding of little Michael's acceptance or rejection of each request because her life experience had always included this belief. Consequently, through practice, the ability to reach deeply into understanding and accepting the infant on his or her terms had been refined by generation after generation of mothers in Ruth's tribe.

Observing Ruth's child rearing techniques and Michael's happy, harmonious growth was a great eye opener for me, a seasoned parent. Over the year and a half that Ruth served as Michael's mother too, we became fast friends. Many moments of enlightenment came to me as Ruth and I sat in her kitchen sipping tea and sharing the experiences of our lives. A significant opportunity for expanding my own views on parenting and living would have been missed by not accepting Ruth just as she was when we had time together. I not only shared in the simple, honest beauty of Ruth, I was able to try new ways of interacting with my baby because of the exchange of beliefs between us. Ruth was a wonderful teacher and a dear friend.

By allowing oneself to develop a style of acceptance of other people, a person also begins to expand the ability to accept other things in life. Since each individual's path in life crosses a multitude of other individual paths, there is a much bigger picture within which each individual contributes and participates. Each life serves as one small strand in a grand tapestry of reality. If the individual has come to a place of simple faith in the universe's desire for balance and harmony, it becomes easy to realize that personal desires may not always align with the picture of the master tapestry. Sometimes the timing is off or the vision of fulfillment is not workable. Often one's sight is not wide enough to recognize what already exists in their life. Replacing the frustration with an expanded method of thinking helps the mind recognize the fulfillment that often comes in ways vastly different than expected. Honoring the uniqueness of each individual also means there is a need for personal give and take and patience. In the loving support of unity each individual serves the growth of the whole community because of the common focus. Benefit to the community equals benefit for each individual as well. Thus the personal desire comes into alignment with the goal of the unified group.

The final stage of many difficult life dramas is acceptance. When grieving a loss one may well pass through shock, anger, denial, and bargaining, but the individual reclaims life and is once again able to move forward when acceptance is achieved. These same stages occur in resolving conflicts, facing serious illness, and establishing one's proper place in many different life experiences. The difficulty generally comes because the vision of self is separate from the unity that is in charge of the tapestry pattern. In order to maintain balance and live life with real purpose, each person needs to recognize and accept with honor their place in the tapestry. As wondrous as human beings are, they are not meant to be the "big brain", but an important strand in an amazing, dynamic miracle—life.

## Chapter 6

# Communication, Gratitude, and Love

Ruth, Michael's other mother, allowed me to see a much deeper, more sensitive communication between Mother and child. Although this is evident in almost every Mother's recognition of different cries for hunger, danger, and sickness, Ruth's communication was conscious and carried the belief that understanding more aspects of the baby's desires and preferences could be developed by anyone. Certainly, as times goes on and the baby grows into a child, parents do come to realize that the child is an individual with their own set of likes and dislikes. But wouldn't it be exciting to participate in a clear, non-verbal exchange with our children at anytime and in any place? The possibilities and benefits are endless. When there is major illness, separation, distress, or some other situation that compromises honest, verbal expression, a comfortable, established connection would be in place.

*Dolores Calley*

On occasion many people use such a link. They hook right in when desperation fills their lives, and they find nowhere else to turn. This communication is commonly called prayer. Whatever name it is given, the exchange is with spiritual, not physical beings. More and more people are breathing life into spiritual exchange through meditation, talking to angels, and praying to God. The difference between present practices and Ruth's connection with Michael is that human beings tend to look outside the species and put faith in "spiritual beings" who do not exist in a body, whereas Ruth suggests that each of us is a spiritual being as well as a human being, and communication without a common language is possible. This practice, developed within the family, can be extended to include the larger brother and sisterhood of humankind. Maybe by communicating with the individual spirits of friends and loved ones, each person would find and welcome the spiritual being within the human body.

The belief that Ruth planted within me took time to grow, but it became a comforting and helpful ability as John and Wendel got older. Teenage years always seem to put a strain on parent-child communication. Wendel's years of desperation certainly crippled an ability to sit down with each other and have an easy chat about our lives. When life with Wendel was most difficult, in my own desperation, I would send Wendel to his bedroom, and I would go into my own room which was next to his. There I would sit on the bed and spill the loving contents of my heart to him. Since I was not quite sure of the proper technique, I would send the thoughts out in words and pictures. These transmissions were meant to remind Wendel of the happy moments we had shared and to allow both of us to come together as we had in the past. In this manner I was able to dump my anger, frustration, and fear, and focus on the love that seemed to be falling like sun sparkled water down a mighty cliff, traveling ever further from the source. In my naiveté, skeptically using the telepathic communication, I hoped to salvage enough of a bond between us to rekindle the closeness that Wendel and I had shared for many years. I believed this was truly possible because my spirit message to Wendel was of the love and gratitude for his presence in my life. Unfortunately, this feeling I had for Wendel now lay neglected beneath angry words and hostile actions. The truth of how I felt had not changed over the course of his childhood. The thing that did change was my ability to express my feelings honestly. I believed Wendel was having the same difficulty. I continued to have an overwhelming desire and need to bring the truth back into my life, and I also hoped that through a continued communication, albeit a strange one, with Wendel, the love and truth would leave a trail for him to follow when his eyes were able to see and accept love again.

An opportunity to try the spirit talk with John came several months later. John had decided to join the Air Force, and the two of us went down for his final processing. The day had been one of long periods of waiting mixed with short momentary gains. John was at his wit's end. He wasn't waiting another minute. He was up on his feet and ready to leave. Calmly I sat, focused on John, and began the silent, mental conversation. "Is this what you truly want to do, John? The wait will end soon. If you want to be in the Air Force, don't throw it away for some frustrating moments that will come to an end."

Within minutes John settled back into the hard plastic chair and sighed. We made it through the day. I felt the communication of spirit to spirit had an impact on the outcome. This was just the beginning of a practice I continue to expand to all manner of things today.

Now I live quite a distance from John and Wendel, so we only see each other twice a year. There are many days in between visits when I wish to be with my grown children. At those times I share what is in my heart with them using the well established "spirit line." In many ways I now feel closer to John and Wendel, and I attribute that closeness to an established spiritual connection. I strongly believe that this new communication, which defies distance and time, has solidified and intensified the relationship I have with each of my children in ways that talking on the phone and visiting never could. I often wonder about the potential of a cooperative exchange where John or Wendel would meet me in the skies somewhere over North America at 6 PM EST on Saturdays. We have a much more supportive family than the family I have known with my mother and siblings. I think that support comes from better communication, especially the heart based kind that carries the light of honesty, the warmth of love, and genuine acceptance.

When communicating by spirit I open my heart. The thoughts I want to share are brought down into my heart before they are sent forth. The heart filtering is one of purifying, transforming the message into an exchange that is free of manipulation and ulterior motives. It is what lies beneath the mountainous heap of judgments, expectation, correct behavior, and proper expression as defined by society's code of conduct. The honesty would be enough, but the love energy of the heart carries each message, and that enhances the thoughts and opens the receiver's heart in acceptance.

Some people are probably wondering if this is just a lot of hogwash. Having been a skeptic myself, I will encourage you to try it yourself. It is safe; no one has to know that you are sending out love-enhanced, honest thoughts to very specific individuals. The assessment for you will only come from your own results. If you are willing to give this technique a try, the following is a simple and often dramatic anger diffuser with which you may want to start. As the frustration is coming at you in a barrage of angry words, begin to silently say, "Only love prevails." No matter what the other person says, do not get sucked into a verbal tussle, focus on the "only love prevails" and then see what comes to you. Express that which has been born out of a loving, sincere focus. If you are pleased with your results, don't stop there!

Children understand spiritual communication much better than adults do. They openly talk to trees, rocks, clouds, dolls and animals, living or stuffed. Often they engage in whole conversations, receiving from as well as sending messages to the other "participant." In addition to talking with other beings, young children often see them. For John, it was the "bogey man"; for Wendel, his deceased grandfather. By observing the child's actions and reactions, it is plain that there is some form of communication going on. My close friend's granddaughter, Gina, of whom my friend had custody, often saw "invisible beings." Initially, one of us would jump up and go to the site with Gina. As this little two year old trembled in terror, the wise adult would emphatically state, "There is no one, absolutely nothing." But the terror remained as Gina shook. The sightings did not diminish until the adults accepted Gina's visions as real and spoke with the apparition, telling it to go away. From watching Gina's little body relax and seeing the carefree smile return, having an adult chase the scary spirit away worked.

Most of the people I know understand little about spirit; I understand little about spirit. This is not unusual because, although learning about the spirit within people has been part of the culture of indigenous peoples, this pursuit has not been a priority for modern, capitalistic society. People who have pursued an understanding of spirit have often been ridiculed and isolated for their crazy ideas, but if an intelligent study of the spirit were actively pursued, maybe people would discover a dimension of being that would allow greater human expression here on earth. Maybe there is an awareness of being and a sense of connectedness associated with all things, but, perhaps this place of unity can best be reached through the human spirit. No one has satisfactorily confirmed or denied the existence of a spiritual being within the body of a human being. So this exploration into the unknown world of spirit is wide open, and, if there are beings who share in the adventures of earth and who know of me, I, for one, would enjoy an exchange of words or thoughts or spiritual energy.

*Awakening Wisdom from Innocence*

Since I have had good success with this silent communication with my children, I have been mind talking to all manner of things, the stars, the sun, the earth, plants, pets and all type of non-living presences in my life. Most often I express my gratitude for the help, beauty, and comfort these things bring into my life. Expressing gratitude does wonders, not only for the recipient, but also for the grateful person. Over time, the sender's focus changes. Where judgment, lack, and separation may have resided, a grateful feeling of appreciation, respect, and connectedness begins to take hold. The individual is adjusting the vision of his or her life to see the service and love extended to him or her by all kinds of things. Thus, the sight begins to focus on all the good things in one's life. Often this optimistic view replaces one of lack and separation. Slowly, a wisdom of the heart, gratitude, is being exercised and validated as a valuable pursuit.

Within society the words "thank you" are taught as though they are to be given out as candy in a classroom of well-behaved students. Real gratitude is a state of being that is reflected in one's approach to all things. Children are born with sincere gratitude. It twinkles like rays of sunshine in the joy of their play and the excitement of discovery. If a child is taught to say thank you for a gift, why isn't the sun remembered and thanked daily for the gift of a new day? Most people would think it crazy to thank a bed for a restful sleep, the hot shower for soothing relaxation, and the car for a safe trip home. But even if these every day items may not hear the words or read the thoughts, by expressing gratitude, the heart (your heart, my heart) begins to wake up the individual's awareness to a view of a world that works in cooperation and love and to the intelligence contained within the heart. This intelligence is a blend of the mind's logic and the body's emotions coming together in the watchful, constant love of the heart. Through the channel of gratitude, spiritual functions of the heart can begin to develop with a directed awareness.

Most people do not think of the heart as having intelligence, but just by looking at the function of the heart, its capabilities are certainly awesome. A limited level of observation may miss the greater potential of such an unconditionally loving and serving organ. For the totality of a life, the heart will send blood, the source of nutrients, communication, and individual essence throughout the body, to every cell, sixty or more times each minute of every hour of every day. The devotion and dedication of the heart to the body and to the individual is selfless, deep, and obviously based on great love. How could the heart not be capable of intelligence?

The heart continues it's constant rhythmic vigilance long after other body systems slow down for rest. The heart is the one that takes on the responsibility for the body even as the mind withdraws to the dream landscape. Even though human declaration generally counts the mind superior, when a person stops and considers the uninterrupted devotion and service of the heart, equality should be awarded. Medically, a person can be brain-dead for a length of time, but I have never heard of heart-dead.

Wisdom is the intelligence of the heart. This revered quality does not necessarily present itself with a pair of spectacles and a long gray beard. Often wisdom is apparent in the clear, searching eyes of a newly born infant, the gentle warmth of a toddler's touch, and the unique commentary about life that spills out of a preschooler's rosy mouth. Since each person has a heart, wisdom is not only within the reach of each person, but a necessary, acquired art of all those who participate in a harmonious unity. Wisdom is merely a matter of choice. Desire is the key to learning the art of wisdom, and this culture is ready to take such a step, one person at a time.

Just as human beings have trained themselves to be intelligent, society could focus on developing the wisdoms of the heart. The brain's thinking is logical, devoid of a moral conscience. Thought processes are computer-like: step A yields result B, and there is no consideration of how other living and non-living things are affected either in the present or the future. Brain focus is on the necessary steps to complete the task at hand; the ends justify the means. Generally when human beings decide upon pursuing an action, the expected outcome is passed through a moral screen, and then a decision to proceed or rethink is made. The process is directed by the mind using the heart wisdom in the capacity of an advisor, not a decision maker. Foreseeing the multileveled ramifications of man's actions has not been a human strong point, because the heart's function of overseeing, harmonizing, and directing with love the actions indicated by the emotions and mind of individuals has not been recognized, nurtured and incorporated. Perhaps now is the time to consciously expand the appreciation of the greater capacity of the human body, suspend the present hierarchy of organs of importance, and explore the depths of the heart. Please try and imagine a world based on such a practice, where the motivating force in all decisions and actions is love, the depths of which modern humanity has yet to experience.

Since cultural values are often contrary to human values, a very popular desire today is for great personal wealth. People avidly play the stock market hoping for a killing that will set them up for life. Recently game shows with big cash prizes have attracted audiences from other programs, and most states have a lottery that attracts a large body of participants. People want riches and enough abundance for all the tomorrows they may face. The logic of the brain chides, "I need a lot now, so that I can still live this "high on the hog" when I get old."

The emotions add their two cents, "Having money, spending money feels wonderful!" But when the individual is faced with a friend who has lost her job or a relative who is forced to spend his

*Dolores Calley*

life's saving on medical bills, the high emotions begin to falter and mix with the sad feelings like vegetables in a soup.

Responding to the new information, the brain, in smug fashion retorts, "That's easy. Let's go for more money, a greater fortune." Remember the logical, devoid-of-feeling functioning of the brain.

Meanwhile, the emotions have had an opportunity to experience a further mixing when their human being works his way up the big business, money-making ladder. Now he is in a position to really affect other people's lives, and he is often called upon to cut staff, combine departments, merge companies, and otherwise impact people's ability to secure their own financial lives. As the emotions come to overload, they begin to hide out in deep areas of the body. Aches and pains start to plague the individual climbing up the ladder to success.

The brain swells with power because it now has free reign and can go into frenzied high gear to secure a fortune and complete the task. The emotions are not happy ones, and the nagging depression, in light of such wealth and success, is confusing. The muffled expression of the ostracized emotions begins to find their outlet in pain, tumors, blockages, and body debilitation. Clearly a mediator is needed to bring balance back to these sibling systems of the body.

All too often the balance and harmony never comes, because success, the indicator of a life's value, is usually equated with money. And the brain has become most efficient at accomplishing the task of amassing money, providing the emotions stay out of the way. The heart beats quietly, continuously, waiting to give the wisdom of love to the being the heart serves. Possibly there is a message in the proliferation of heart disease; possibly the reminder is to stop neglecting the heart, stop dismissing love.

If the heart joins the scenario between the brain and the emotions, the picture has to change dramatically, such that, first the individual changes and then society changes. The basis for change is established. With time a new culture is born. The brain will still be called upon to develop a plan of action and the feedback of the emotions will guide the direction. The heart will provide the nourishment, communication, and individual essence as usual, and that equals action based on love. This time the individual will be able to see this world within the framework of a bigger existence and understand the sustaining force of the heavens. The individual will see money as a means of exchange for the items necessary to fulfill human desires and support participation in the creation of a satisfying life. The heart would provide a communication that says all are united in one body, on one earth, and thus, either equally lacking or equally living in abundance. Understanding and functioning from this belief, competition is exchanged for co-operation.

As the individual goes forth with this information, the brain's plan for abundance will have to employ methods that bring others up the ladder, instead of gaining personal riches in a rush for the top rung by stepping on the backs and fingers of fellow workers. Emotional feedback from the gratitude of those who move in the wave of abundance that pours forth from the individual's sea of love will confirm and support the brain's plan. The emotional response will encourage the brain to seek ways to extend the abundance to include support for others in their expression and manifestation of abundant creativity. Generations later the comfort of having needs meet would be a given, no longer a continuing challenge in life. There would not be an elite few at the top of the ladder; everyone would be at the top.

There would be authentic community without the centralized power of wealth. Humanity would then be able to focus on truth, beauty, love and other lofty pursuits.

Not that any of this is easy to accomplish, but exploring the possibility is the first step to bringing the idea into actuality. And once again, people have the power. Culture is a choice. The individuals who make up the society create the society as they create their lives and their reality. This beautiful picture of society is just a choice away. Indigenous peoples have provided various templates. Developing the capabilities of the heart is a possible doorway into a consciously directed wondrous future.

Children know of love. The little ones are often earth's biggest, continuous source of love. Somehow, as children grow, the love they so freely understood and practiced becomes confused and scattered. Their overflowing spring of love evaporates under the pressures of cultural impositions and parents who have succumbed to and continue to teach by example that monetary pursuits are the important ones.

Writing about love is difficult because love has been played around with so much that it is difficult to find a deep, sustaining expression of love, the type of image one can look at and say, "Ah, love." Is it love in Internet chat rooms, divorce and remarriage, same sex unions, and many other variations on the theme of love? In this modern culture love is often synonymous with sex, and when pornography and child molestation seep into the picture, one has to wonder where love is, or if people are even capable of real love.

Wendel helped me uncover love within myself. He gave me the opportunity to realize I could share my love with others, even when they did not appear to want love. Most of my family saw Wendel as a lost cause. Doctors had no real answers except for medication and time. John, Wendel, and I lived in an environment that was permeated with despair, isolation, and pain. Out of this void, I experienced a truer essence of the kind of love that flowed from an abundant spring that was pure, strong, and prevailing. Funny how the most desperate times bring forth the most dramatic hope just as the winter holds the promise of spring. A belief in the power of love was all that I had left. I think that the hope rode on the back of spirit, shimmering through the swamp as my defenses fell in a battle of survival. Weakened by the struggle, love was able to move in and fill the empty places. No longer attached to old beliefs that were not working, I was susceptible to the love that had been waiting to entice new believers.

With Wendel there was one thing I knew; he truly needed someone to love him just as he was with no expectations, judgments, or demands. The love had to be freely given, and I could not expect any kind words, thoughtful actions, or affectionate hugs in return. I would have to find my own fountain of love because I required abundant love, enough for John, me, and especially Wendel. But isn't this the kind of love each of us seeks? Isn't the expectation, the desire for love that lasts forever and that lives beyond time and space, sought by all? What do you think; does such love exist somewhere? Is it of this world?

Interestingly, as I write about love, I am working at an alternative school, a place where the kids with problems go for their education. The very evident difficulties include trouble with the law, pregnancy, drug abuse, and other societal flaws. These blossoming adults remind me of Wendel in their struggle to find a place in an adult world that says, "you do not fulfill expectations, there really is no place for you here." In many ways the modern adult world, which holds the pattern of society firmly in place, has produced these outcast children, robbing them of acceptance, denying them a loving, supportive, and safe place to express who they are and explore their unique life perspective. The basis for this life sentence is judgment. Comparison is to a social norm, and the turned backs and labels that declare them unacceptable, execute their isolation. In a loving community this would be unlikely to happen. These young members of society need love, just as Wendel needed unconditional love. Unfortunately, as these youth are subjected to increasing isolationism, they mistrust the gift of love. Their teenage years often become a serious, intense time for them, and those who love them.

I have to ask myself why has life brought me to this school, back to flounder in this painful expression of life? I have been here before very directly with my own child, and I have felt small and useless. To find an answer, I have to go higher, find a more expanded picture and view the scene from a perspective of compassionate detachment. The understanding and resolve for big issues rarely comes from the level where things are happening because the individual is too close. There is a great need to employ an objective focus and look at the larger framework when one seeks an answer that will explain the pain and bring truth to the greater experience of life. The resolve occurs when one returns to the lower level and implements action based on the information gained from a bigger picture and an objective viewpoint.

When I put this powerful tool to use, developed from my own struggle, I find that these children are my sisters and brothers. They, like me, speak of the need for change in a society that is squeezing the very spirit out of too many people subjected to restrictive rules and the denial of love. These young people, with their very lives, call upon each of us to transform the struggle on earth by finding and living love. To me, the task is worth a massive effort, because I long to know who these members of my extended family really are. I want to be able to laugh with them and celebrate their accomplishments and unique perspective. I know that interacting with one another does not have to be so difficult.

Love in the society may be difficult to find and define in a clear manner, but love is evident in the natural world. Love is so present that people no longer recognize love's presence. It is taken for granted, just like the air that one breathes, the sun that will reappear each day bringing warmth and light, the abundance of life-sustaining water that will recycle itself, and the call of night's darkness that will bring rest. All of these ever-present requirements of human life are held in place by love, but these real images of love have been supplanted by the images of consumerism. If you look at the human response to these gifts of life, one can hardly deny that human beings are polluting the air, poisoning the water, running from the sun, and carrying light into the night so that work can continue. Somehow, I do not think that I would use the words gratitude and appreciation as a summation of the human response to the gift of love that sits ever ready to infuse the human race. This unconditional love could carry humanity well beyond these basic gifts and serve as an example for human relationships.

From now on I will try and put forth ever-growing love, simply because it is a place to start. Diminishing judgment, incorporating expanded thinking modes, and communicating gratitude for all things in my life will encourage my transformation. The choice to change will bring forth my potential as a human and spiritual being, align me

*Awakening Wisdom from Innocence*

to my true purpose in life, and minimize fear. The next step will be to realize my personal power and use that strength to move closer to a unity with all expressions of love on earth, to uncover and live by truth and respect for the gift of being present and participating in the moments I have been given. Thus, I will move toward an exploration of truth. I will let you in on a little secret. I have been dreading this look at truth. I have been searching for a way to avoid dealing with truth. I hope someone out there identifies with me.

## Chapter 7

# Truth, Personal Power, & Responsibility

Please understand, I like truth. I believe in truth, but I will admit that I often have a hard time discerning the truth. In high school I had a very tall and jolly boyfriend. He loved practical jokes and my gullibility. To explain how naive I can be, I will tell you this embarrassing true story, complete with gullible young girl and jolly boyfriend. During the sixties the East Coast of the United States was experiencing severe drought. This went on for a few years. Every summer my family would take a much anticipated summer vacation. One year we decided to go to Niagara Falls in upstate New York. When my boyfriend heard about the destination, he said, "Gee, it is a shame you are going to Niagara Falls this year, because they have to dam up the falls. You know, there's a drought, and we have all got to conserve water."

I retorted, "Nobody can do that, dam up a waterfall. You're putting me on, aren't you?"

*Awakening Wisdom from Innocence*

"No, they really close this big dam across the whole falls every night." he replied emphatically. "It helps save the water. Shame you're going <u>this</u> year."

Hesitantly, my confidence dwindling, "Are you sure? Maybe my family should go someplace else."

"I wouldn't lie to you, honest."

Needless to say, as I stood looking at the falls from a window in the restaurant, no dam appeared, the falls continued to spill in their awesome magnificence. As night descended and robbed my view, the warm redness shot up my neck warming my face. I don't recall whether the emotion was anger or embarrassment, but the final result was laughter. I remember that tall, happy guy for all the laughter we shared, and most of the time we were laughing at the outrageous things I would wholeheartedly swallow as truth.

Around the same time in my life, I really wanted to know all those secret, grown-up truths. If, in my teenage ignorance, I could quickly understand those truths, I could smoothly find my happily-ever-after and move into the peaceful life I saw on the Hollywood big screen. Little did I realize how elusive the truth, especially of one's own life, could be. This teenage quest for the truth continues, but the picture of what I am looking for has had several transformations.

The only truth I feel confident about is change. Whatever is going on will inevitably drift away and be replaced with something different. Truth does not layer itself neatly like the little bricks in a solid wall. Truth is much more like a compost pile. The gardener layers the fresh green garden remnants, followed by the dried up brown yard debris and some dirt. Somewhere along the way, heat, water, bugs, bacteria, chemical changes, and time mix the layers. What was once smelly rotting organic waste, becomes rich, sweet-smelling soil waiting to nourish dainty little seeds and bring forth their potential to become giant trees, beautiful flowers, and scrumptious vegetables. As in a person's life, family, friends, career, location, experience, and time come together and contribute to the truth of one's life, and bring forth or limit the individual's potential.

Sometimes the compost blend sours and smells. The gardener needs to turn it, aerate the mass, or add different stuff so that the process can proceed. Life is often like that, and one needs to change careers or a new friend comes along. Maybe a new baby adds to the

*Awakening Wisdom from Innocence*

family or someone dies. The truth of the person's life shifts, parts break away or come together, once again rebuilding and nourishing the creativity and sparking the imagination.

The everyday truth by which an individual lives expands, contracts, and alters. This truth is pliable, shaping itself out of the experiences of the moment, collecting memories like old photographs. I like to think of this manifestation of truth as the practical, applicable-to-life truth. This truth guides people through their lives by providing a basis for the actions, reactions, and decisions that are part of an individual's path. As the level of earth experience grows, the truth changes using the new information to refine, enhance, and serve the continuing experience of living.

The best compost piles include a healthy amount of dirt, and I equate this constant, earth-to-soil portion of the compost, as those other unalterable, constant truths that often frustrate individuals seeking a stable, unchanging life. A permanent truth was exactly the truth my teenage self sought. I would use that as a basis for a wonderful life. I spent years looking for the stability of a reliable answer, the key truth to the good life. This did not seem attainable to a simple, small person like me. I felt that if I could find and live that truth, my marriage would be filled with love and happiness, my children would delight in impressive obedience and appropriate growth toward success, and my work would be a source of personal pride and service to humanity. This is where the addition of the earth to the compost pile brings continuity. The soil added to the compost equals the constant truths: love conquers all, do unto others, turn the other cheek, time heals all wounds, and other lofty aspirations. These are but a part of the truths needed to live life day-by-day, just as soil is but a part of the compost pile.

The constant truths serve not only the experience of life on earth, but also the universal, cosmic picture that includes angels, spirits, and other beings. Thus, this truth needs to be very simple, and often life within a cultural framework is complex. The spiritual aspect of being human undoubtedly lives by such stable truths, but within the framework of a society, carrying all the restraints and dictates of a social structure, the constant truths are not always workable, realistic, or easy to live by. I expect that each person has an internal drive that inevitably pushes him or her to seek ways to bring these truths down

*Awakening Wisdom from Innocence*

to a practical expression here on earth. I believe this to be natural. Indigenous cultures do this, I feel, with what one might call a heightened consciousness or intuitively. Part of the mission of <u>each</u> human being is to uncover the eternal truths and give them definition through life lived based on love. And if each person on earth were shining the truth of love through the example of their life, what brilliance would be sent forth from earth into the cosmos. Since much of what is demanded by society is alien to the spiritual aspect of being human, the challenge to anchor the constant truths on earth is great.

In a perfect world the constant truth and the day-to-day truth would be in alignment. Then the truth of love would sparkle through everyone's actions and reactions. There would be no need for laws, wars, or policemen. Disciplining children would hardly be necessary. But this is not the case. Yet, underlying normal family interactions is the eternal truth of love even when it is hard to perceive. If a child is rude, belligerent, and uncooperative, one might question the belief that love is the basis of family interaction. One might feel that there is a lack of love in both the behavior of the child, who will say hurtful words and fail to contribute to the household in a positive way, and the parent, who will take abuse from the child or assert unnecessary power. Somewhere along the path of life, the manifestation of the basic truth of love has been hidden from this family. The unalterable truth is there, but it is under a mountain of other assumptions, (some may call them truths) which relate directly to a human experience, often minus the spiritual interpretation of love. They include ideas like: I am the child, so I get all the love no matter what I do; people will think I am a bad parent if I discipline my child; if he or she loved me they would not do that, and all the other earthly parameters used to assess the "proper" expression of love between people.

The scene between parent and child becomes one of power, not love. The struggle is one of domination and control of the will of the other person. One sometimes sees the same power play between individuals and the government. Both parent and child are indulging in a game of fortifying or dismantling the social structure of modern society. I do not really believe that any child sets out to be obnoxious, rude, or difficult. These misfit behaviors are created by rules shaped to extract obedience to choiceless demands, to submit to constant assessment against often undefined standards, and to yield without questioning to other arbitrary requirements. The expression of love by the parent is disciplining the child to help ensure that the child can find a secure and successful place in their adult role within the society. The child's love is displayed by indicating the need to revise aspects of the society that are causing suffering to some members of the community.

When the parent forces appropriate behavior through punishment, the child's response may be, "screw you." And in the child's reply comes a resounding statement that says; I am not playing this game. The child is asserting his or her right to reject the society's demand of being molded as a dutiful consumer and worker. He or she plainly reveals a feeling of not being heard, and he or she expresses pain, now disguised as anger and resentment. Love is the underlying thread, but it is caught in a web of predetermined roles, expectations, community beliefs and rules, conflicting emotions, self-doubt, and mistrust. There is no wrong or right without a standard of comparison, and in this case the standard is based upon the society's code of conduct for both the child and the adult. When one looks at the power of this code of conduct, it plainly is on the rise, and the expression of love suffers greater compromise at each step. Today, parents are often held accountable in a court of law for the behavior of their child. The court is supporting, even demanding, the power struggle interaction over the love-based relationship. The ramifications can be severe for the parent who does not stand as a pillar holding up the structure of the society, even at the expense of love.

Most of the conflict with truth winds it's way back to the challenges of expressing the magnificent spirit of the individual within the confining structure of modern western culture. Uncovering the truth of each life and finding a way to live that truth within the parameters of modern society is one of the most difficult quests every person faces. The choice is adjusting the truth to fit the community structure or changing the societal structure to reflect the truth. More often than not, the truth is compromised to accommodate the society's position. Standing up for truth, especially when truth is in conflict with cultural dictates, can cause immense hardships in a person's life. But if one desires a sparkling clarity in his or her life, the individual will have to honor and support the truth. Since free will is a right of each individual, anyone can choose truth in any circumstance, at any time. Often the choice of truth encourages lessons in courage and honor.

An individual's authentic personal power is called into action by free will in the choices one makes. And there is <u>always</u> a choice. A person's view of the circumstances, all too often, is so narrowly boxed in by laws, unwritten codes of conduct, and expectations that the individual can no longer see the choices present in the dense fog of predetermined political requirements, social correctness, and uncompromising faith in an authority on any given subject.

Part of the reason people in today's society do not even recognize that there is a choice, is because over the years individuals have been slowly handing over aspects of personal responsibility to an outside agency. One is no longer qualified to address his or her own health concerns; there are well-trained physicians to do that. That "modern truth" is repeated in many important areas of life including the education of children, the dispersion of salaried funds, personal spiritual growth, family priorities, and many other areas of life. Some years ago people started specializing in very narrowly defined careers. Employable skills became highly specific and focused in multiple areas within the same general category. For example, within the field of laboratory medicine, I went from doing laboratory testing in most departments of the laboratory including Chemistry, Hematology, Urinalysis, Microbiology, and Serology, to specializing in only one department. As skills compartmentalized, people recognized the highly trained abilities of others to advise them in particular areas of their life. Coincidentally, money was exchanged for services and advice that further established an economy-driven world as the appropriate way to live. As this process continued individuals began to accept the educated authority as superior to their own choice in personal matters. This process has progressed to a dangerous place. Doctors take on the responsibility for health, teachers for the education of children, government for rules of appropriate behavior, lawyers as debate settlers, and the list for relinquished responsibilities fulfilled by outside sources in exchange for money continues. Parenting has also been doled out to experts who often do not even have children.

Unfortunately, many people feel inadequate when it comes to making very important decisions that will dramatically affect their lives. Embracing such a belief supports an inability to even realize that other choices are available in a given situation. If I believe that the physician is much more competent in restoring my health than I am, when I am diagnosed with breast cancer, I will surrender the choice of treatment to the doctor. The doctor will not have to directly live with the results of the decision, I will. And if I have deferred my free will, failed to exercise my personal power, I can hold someone else accountable for a poor outcome. This belief has led to the rise of a victim mentality, a prosperous insurance industry, an abundance of lawyers, and a continuing erosion of faith in one's self as well as in one another. For many individuals this erosion of faith includes faith in God or the spiritual world as well. Perhaps one can look upon the belief in a Supreme Being as a "relinquished responsibility." Of course, taking up the cloak of victimhood is not totally accurate because a choice has been made if I were to choose to allow someone else to make my decision. I am still responsible, even though I have set myself up to cower and cry under the blanket of victimization. What I am really doing is refusing to accept responsibility and refusing to exert my own personal power. The sad fact is that due to over-intellectualization of aspects of life, one sometimes does have difficulty in making a sensible choice. There is a frenetic deluge of information, often conflicting, on any subject which impacts life. Thus, one finds it very easy to defer decision, to continue the erosion of confidence, and to avoid acceptance of responsibility.

Women especially suffer from this deferment syndrome because they have been raised to yield to the desires of their husbands and other male authority figures. Modern culture is based on patriarchy and male dominance. I believe the trend to change the image of women in today's society has been aided by all those single mothers with the primary responsibility for the children they have been raising alone. My most significant moments of discovering my personal power came from the dark years with Wendel. During this time I had to make some very serious decisions with little support from anyone. Because of Wendel's destructive and sometimes bizarre behavior, friends and family suggested committing him to a psychiatric hospital for long-term care. That was not acceptable to me and provided a strong impetus to stand firmly alone in a blizzard of criticism. In my mind, the medical people involved offered conflicting and inadequate advice on what needed to be done to help Wendel. Often I was alone with trust and personal power as my horse and shield. Both served me well and remain ready to support me again. Because of trust and personal power, Wendel, even with bizarre and destructive behavior, was given the opportunity to grow through his pain and establish his own comfortable and productive place in society.

Once personal power is discovered, the owner has the strength of choice, the power of directing his or her own life. He or she will not easily relinquish it. Personal power makes a person strong and confident. Personal power erases victimhood because the individual realizes that the choice is his or hers even if the choice is to disregard the matter or yield the decision to someone else. In accepting the right and freedom to choose, one begins to understand the responsibility that is wrapped tightly around each decision made.

When a person truly understands and accepts the responsibility for his or her actions and decisions, that individual voluntarily assumes the consequences of each action taken. The individual learns responsibility because, through acceptance, they either suffer the results of poor decisions or reap the benefit of successful choices.

Since each individual has the underlying current of love running through his or her being, the individual will find the greatest degree of harmony in making choices that will reflect love. And the reflection of love brings one back to honoring the truth, especially the deep abiding spiritual ones that grow out of love. A hint to knowing if a choice is aligned with love comes from ease in following through with action. The individual may feel like the steps to accomplishing the goal are flowing, that many things are joining to complete the mission.

Responsibility, in it's purest form, comes from a source of self-love. Because one loves himself or herself, the choices made will be in the interest of the highest good for the individual. When a person has come to a point of self-love, there is an understanding and source of love that flows outward in interaction with others. The interaction no longer presents selfish demands or needs to the other people in the individual's life. As one meets his or her own requirements for a fulfilling life, the individual develops a sense of worth and confidence. These good feelings continue to be fed through the utilization of personal power in making decisions that honor the truth of the beliefs the individual carries within his or her being. Having achieved a high level of individualization, the individual can then decide, using the power of free will, to join or co-create a cooperative unity.

The most obvious expression of love within many cultures is marriage. I believe the physical attraction between a man and woman is strong, often irresistible, to encourage the human exploration of a cooperative unity. Within the small circle of two, formed because of the powerful pull of love, the partners can hone the skills needed for the harmonious unity of thinking beings. Some of the skills include sharing, compromise, and truthful communication. At the time two people decide to enter into a partnership, they have made a commitment to the creation of a new, two-part unity, and thus, transfer personal responsibility to the unity of their marriage.

In the ideal situation there is an adjustment period before the circle of a wedded partnership grows into a family as children are born. If the transition period has allowed strong individuals to adapt responsibility, desire, and focus to the new oneness, a secure, loving foundation for the expansion to a family will naturally occur. And in this ideal situation the solid foundation will be the base for a cooperative structure that moves on to an ever-growing unity that comes to include the community, world, and universe. Many people are striving for a place in such a world.

Obviously, when one looks at divorce rates, single parent households, and a variety of family descriptions, the ideal is far from a regular occurrence. Instead, there are many attempts, and consequently, a plethora of models from which to work. What does unite these different family groupings is the opportunity to discover within the individual and families techniques and beliefs about cooperative unity. This ability to work harmoniously with one another for the good of all requires the expansion of personal responsibility to the family.

Even though many families fall apart, individuals are afforded opportunities to refine their beliefs about creating and functioning within a unified group. There are also dramas that encourage lessons of responsibility in the aftermath of a family break up. All too often the children are used as tools for punishment, self indulgence, and power plays, when, in fact, the innocent players should be given the greatest consideration. Often, their knowledge of what is happening is faulty because their understanding of how the culture works is lacking. Years after my first divorce, I talked with John and Wendel. We spoke about their personal feelings about divorce from their father. Wendel was two years old at the time of the divorce. He used to chase men in the supermarket declaring, "I found him! I found my father."

When the boys and I spoke years later, Wendel said that he knew if he were smart enough, his dad would come back. Wendel attended a private school for his early elementary education. During his year in first grade he completed first, second, and half of third grade. A conclusion, based on a two-year-old's perception of the events in his life, was obviously carried into his early school experience. Perhaps a large portion of the despair of his teenage years was also related to the truths of his life at age two. Wendel's experience strongly indicates that the adults going through divorce need to focus on their responsibility to the continued well-being of the children involved. They are major players in the divorce drama.

*Dolores Calley*

The answer to resolving a family break-up amicably lies in the reliable truth of love. The wisdom of the innocence of the children is again awaiting ears to hear, eyes to see, and hearts to respond. They continue to love both parents and to yearn for time and interaction with mother and father. The responsibility of the parents lies in recognizing this innocent desire, overcoming personal agendas through strengthening their own individuality, and developing a workable communication and relationship with each other. In the long run a loving effort in resolving this difficult drama, divorce, benefits all participants.

Divorce is but one area of life in which modern human beings fail to come together as strong individuals with a sense of commitment and responsibility to one another. There are many bureaucracies that form the intricate web of agencies that compose governments such as the complex one governing America. Since individuals who form these organizations fail to commit with responsibility their talents to these agencies, the bureaucracies often seem to take on a life of their own. As people move into the twenty-first century, these halls, which include health, education, welfare, foreign relations, treasury, legislature, and so on, and which are supposed to function within the cultural guidelines, are lacking the equivalent of a human heart. In comparing these bureaucracies to a human being, they are akin to ego, pure ego that has taken over by selectively sharing information and ignoring emotional feedback. The agencies can put forth an agenda of it's own because it stands alone, lacking the commitment of love and responsibility the members should provide. The people also stand separately by working, quite literally, for personal gain. Each individual who devotes an amazing amount of time and energy to the continuing ability of one of these major foundations of society to function, withholds a personal commitment of responsibility to oversee that the tasks are in the best interest of the unified population. In fact, the individuals within the organization often feel like victims of the systems themselves.

Taken one step further, as members of the society, each individual also has a responsibility for each decision made within the community of members. Throwing up one's hands in frustration is a choice in exercising one's personal power; relinquishing responsibility is also one of the choices. As one can see, such a choice can lead to pollution of the environment, drugging children for compliance, the development and use of very destructive weapons, a quest for riches no matter what the cost, subjugation of people, the death of children at the hands of children, and other oozing sores of modern culture.

Although I have never tried this, I understand that when "cooking" frogs, one needs to put the living frogs into a pot of cool water and slowly raise the temperature. Once the water gets nice and warm, the unsuspecting frogs will become lethargic and complacent, no longer able to summon the energy to jump out of the pot. Many individuals in society seem to be at this point, ready to accept the fate of being cooked alive, and they have not yet resolved their view of death. What those within the pot fail to see or accept is that they are also the cooks turning up the heat. There is an amazing wealth of personal power ready to unite in a common cause when the individuals in the pot realize their other role as cook. At any time they can choose to arrest the process and unite their energies to find a way out of the pot, the pot that is the continuing restrictive structure of a society that is not healthy. Once they accomplish the task of freeing themselves, they can chose to find or construct a beautiful

*Awakening Wisdom from Innocence*

pond in which to wile away their days and rear their young. This peaceful pond scene is possible, but those falling asleep in the pot need to wake up and summon the strength of their courage and live the honor of their beliefs.

# Chapter 8

# Honor, Courage, and Respect

If one has focused deeply upon his or her creative potential, followed the beat of his or her truth with a trusting innocence, overcome fear, expectations, and judgment, moved ever closer to unity and acceptance, discovered how to truly love, and taken on the responsibility for all actions and decisions, this person is living a life of honor. This special one undoubtedly has come to honor their own being and all other creatures and facets of life on earth. Many people are walking this path because this is what life is about, learning the spiritual truths of love and living a life that honors these truths. The dramas and comedies of life are enacted to discover, follow, and share who the person is, what that person honestly comes to believe, and how that specific set of beliefs and creative potential can be brought into the service of others, human and non-human.

As presented in this collection of thoughts and observations, modern society does not generally support a person's efforts to accomplish this task. But how a culture will function is a joint decision that can be changed! Perhaps even beyond supporting the individual in acquiring an authentic stance of honor, modern society has been throwing stones into people's paths. As illustrated by the very earth herself, these stones have turned into boulders, mudslides, lava, and floods. For children, such a situation is especially grave and difficult because they come to us with an innocent and untainted sense of honor expressed through their wonderment and delight at the beautiful world to which they awaken. Those who grow into being within a body already polluted with despair have less of a chance of the societal picture of a successful journey of discovery and service. Their life must be an ongoing nightmare with no devoted family to hold, support, and comfort them. Perhaps the greatest service of those children of the cultural nightmare is in holding up the mirror of truth to society through their sometimes hostile and defiant acts, asking someone to please change the picture.

At the birth of America three virtues were set forth to be honored by the people. They were "life, liberty, and the pursuit of happiness." Indeed, they remain as very noble and desirable undertakings. Over the two hundred plus years of America's existence, honor has combined with other words and taken on a new face which presents the people with honor roll, honor guard, honor society, honor a debt, and receive honors. Judges are referred to as the "Honorable." Obviously, the growth of America has altered that which the people are expected to honor. In this modern age, the people are to honor intellectual achievement, obedience, money, and the laws of man.

Ironically, America was founded because people desired religious freedom. If one looks at capitalism as a religion with money as the godhead, obedience, academic achievement, and the law of man assure that all members will join the church or suffer the consequences of law. In California, the passage of Proposition 21, which will try more juveniles as adults, the "law of man" is being thrust upon young individuals well before they have a chance to even explore who they are or what they believe. Combine this with drug therapy and there is a major attempt to remake spirit, the essence of who one is, as a man-made product, the ultimate product of society. When this occurs, individuals hand their free will over to society because the individual has accepted programming that replaces

*Awakening Wisdom from Innocence*

freedom of choice with cultural dictates. The quest of self-discovery is over or at minimum extremely challenging. I do not believe that any person was meant to represent the perfect societal picture of a man or woman.

The honor of a person, if one can call it that becomes obedience, the pursuit of marketable talents, and a life of playing by rules in which one may not believe. By looking at major problems within the culture (violence, depression, disease, and so on), honoring such goals comes with a very heavy price tag. The man-made stamp, which is structurally based, cannot be put on the human spirit because there is little truth, love, or honor associated with such a goal of society. The immortal aspect of human beings, spirit, is excluded from the goal of being. Aside from that, the authentic human spirit is powerful and desires expression. Thus, the conflict between the nature of being human and lifestyle will seek a resolution.

Every member of society would do well to consciously decide if his or her honor and all that honor includes, is best utilized in continuing to pursue "the American dream" or if that personal honor lies in the discovery of his or her own, individual dream based on his or her own creative potential and brought forth to serve a dynamic and growing culture.

Realizing that society truly changes as individuals and their beliefs change, one can accomplish the immense task of choosing to build a new culture by carefully choosing what to honor and how to follow up with action in one's life to affect the change. Since I personally have a great deal of faith in the human spirit, I believe everything needed for the rise of a remarkable, loving, cooperative, and unified civilization is readily available within us, one individual awakening and changing at a time. I even believe that the prize is a lot easier to attain then anyone thinks. I understand that there are those awaiting salvation in a spaceship filled with enlightened beings or the return of Jesus Christ. Another option lies in accessing the greatness within people who have learned how to avail themselves of the sometimes-overlooked guidance that dwells within their being and the earth.

For me, yesterday was an exceptional day, filled with little miracles. I found myself alone for the whole day, a remarkable occurrence in itself. Since I was not at all pleased with the writing I had done on this chapter, using my spirit communication, I asked whomever, whatever, to help me understand honor so that I could share my insight with those who read this book.

The garden responded in the sparkling sunshine, vivid colors, and musical birdsong of an unexpected spring day. My efforts, at the urging of spirit talk with members of the garden community, were directed to fertilizing the trees and grape plants with compost from grass-covered piles that had been sitting, doing their thing for two years. Following the hard work of breaking down the piles to collect the treasure below, I had to drag the wheelbarrow full of compost up an incline to the awaiting plants. The physical work was hard and an intensifying pain in my back dulled the pleasure of working in the garden. In frustration at the growing limitation, I laid down on the grass surrendering to the warmth of the sun and said, "This work would be much more fun without the pain in my back."

Five minutes later the pain was gone. I, received generous relief, and was able to accomplish much more than I thought was possible. As I worked, I sent thoughts of love to the trees, honoring their presence and hoping to help heal the trees that were struggling from disease last year. At the pear tree I felt a crippling cramp in my diaphragm. So once again I was flat on my back on the grass covered earth. My right hip almost always draws my attention with varying degrees of pain. As I lay uncomfortably on the bumpy incline, warmth filled the hip area generating a release of stress and pain in my hip. Once I rose to my feet again, I proceeded to complete my garden work. I distantly thought that I was walking a little differently, but basically set aside the experience. As I entered the house, I realized the nagging ache had moved to a new place in the hip. Not long afterward, the pain was gone. A delightful five hours had flown by in cooperative unity in the garden. As we honored each other, the plants had brought me to a greater perfection of myself, blending physical, mental, emotional, and spiritual aspects. This realization came only as I awoke the next morning in wonderful health and began to write. All I did to have this special day was to ask about honor. Anyone can do the same: ask, honor, be open to receive, and accept with gratitude.

The natural world seems to be waiting for a loving, mutually honoring participation from human beings. The plants and humans would heal quickly. Nature will often take the human gesture of planting trees or gardens and contribute her own effort in bringing forth beauty and renewal. Response from honoring and working in cooperation with the natural world is certainly not limited to plants and gardening. There are dolphins that heal physical and emotional problems for people. Cats and dogs help people overcome loneliness. The general response from nature to a union based on mutual honor and respect brings forth benefits for all involved. By contrast, if one holds their personal honor within society, the individual is often detained and denied freedom by the government. This cultural response, so alien to the natural world, again indicates that this modern society of human beings is not aligned with the truths of the natural world. A restructuring of the culture, based on spiritual truth, can only improve the way people honor themselves and each other. Honoring one's truth within modern society often requires courage.

Courage is generally associated with soldiers and warriors. Medals are awarded for bravery when one achieves victory in the face of danger. Although this is the popular picture of courage, there is an individual side to courage. For some people, courage is needed to arise and face another day. A child may display courage on the very first day of school, or when saying no to the offer of drugs. Leaving an abusive marriage with little more than the children is also a courageous act. Courage in the examples above is based on overcoming fear. But there is a deeper aspect of courage that comes without fear.

The word courage comes from the Latin "cor", heart. The French "corage" is also rooted in "cuer", heart. Courage is based in the heart because if one's thoughts and emotions have come together in harmony and the understanding of spiritual truths, the heart is peaceful. At the essence of courage is the absence of fear. An individual radiating the epitome of courage knows he or she is immortal and indestructible. This individual accepts his or her role in a challenging drama because a responsibility to the greater good is carried in the person's heart.

The ultimate historical example would be Jesus Christ delivering himself into the hands of the crucifiers. If one believes Biblical accounts, when soldiers came, Christ did not resist. Earlier in the garden he prepared himself, knowing a difficult ordeal was before him. Through the questioning by his captors, crowning of thorns, carrying the cross, the spirit of Jesus Christ was not broken. Even as he hung from the cross, Jesus cried out, "Father forgive them. They know not what they do."

Jesus displayed courage that must have generated from his heart. His words indicate that Jesus knew something more than those who were crucifying him. Jesus was firmly based in life beyond death. He recognized his own immortality. He knew the crucifixion was a vehicle that would take him back to the Father. There is evidence that Jesus Christ consciously chose to participate in this drama, and that he accepted his role. Christ was motivated by his devotion to the greater good and his love of humanity. Like Christ, individuals can understand the greater good, align to a larger truth, and courageously accept their roles in life. An interesting side note to this human drama is that even though Jesus Christ was not a celebrated, titled ruler, carried no reputation as a wealthy man, or left no physical contribution behind, the impact of his life and death has and continues to affect the lives of more people than any other documented person in recorded history. His courage and love continue to echo through humanity.

The echo resonates in the hearts of those who are ready to take on the challenge of unconditional love, the courage of living a life that is aligned with the courage of one's convictions, and the unconditional honor of all. And this combination of the perfection of love, courage, and honor can be the choice of guidance to carry people forth in the next millennium, to help discern what is true and beneficial, and to find the way for change to bring greater peace and happiness to all people. Courage is the first step because rebuilding a societal template modeled on a loving, supportive, cooperative unity requires the de-structuring of many aspects of the present system. And this is a system with gnarled, entwined roots that have dug deeply into the earth.

Change is a reality that many people fear. Remember that the one truth I felt sure of was change. Death also brings forth change. This fear of change and death has isolated and crippled people for far too long. This fear has often charted the course for modern society. Choosing fear as the foundation of a society has to inevitably bring about the downfall. A society based on fear is no longer under the direction of the individuals in the group. The path comes from forces or beliefs outside the group. If people are to join together and rebuild society, courage in accepting change is necessary. For modern society, freedom can once again be practiced when the members have resolved their personal fear of change and the death—life conflict. Courage is knowing in your heart that death is an illusion and personal growth and self-awareness come via the process of change.

There has been no previous period in my lifetime when aspects have come together so well to allow such a conscious choice to be successful on such a massive scale. The actions and obvious problems children are having point very specifically to areas in the culture that need review and correction. These unbalanced aspects include limiting human potential to predominately intellectual achievement, assessing people with a standard which denies an appreciation and validation of strength in diversity, pigeonholing and isolating individuals or groups of people because of judgments and expectations, promoting fear, defining a person's value by the size of their financial holdings, and supporting a pyramid of abundance which uses the masses at the bottom, robbing them of their rights and limiting their access to the levels above, so that they will continue in the increasingly difficult labor of supporting the few at the top.

Courageous creators of a kinder social structure are out there, part of the society, experimenting with new ways of living. They are presently refining aspects of varying models of loving, supportive, cooperative unities. These courageous people include home schooling families who seek ways to bring forth the unique, creative potential of young people, those who have often left successful, corporate lives to return to a daily interaction with the natural world, people who explore ways of providing heat and light to their homes that does not come with a monthly bill or a harmful environmental impact, groups of people who meet to call forth peace and harmony on earth through prayer and action, communities that have developed their own currency and economy which values each individual's work equally, and others who are grounding love, trust, and respect. These creative pioneers who seek a more personally and environmentally friendly life, often do so at the expense of their friends, financial security, and social acceptance. Still their numbers are growing, and their presence means that the change has begun in earnest. They serve as examples of what other living options are available, how life goes on even when one ventures outside the established perimeters of society, and where creativity in lifestyle can begin to stretch and alter present cultural trends. These innovators are courageous, and although one may not agree with some of their changes, their unique lifestyles warrant consideration. Since they are "walking the talk", they deserve respect for looking at a big, complicated structure and bravely moving beyond just believing the present society can be improved. They clear the debris for a new path.

The bureaucratic, governmental response to the inevitable change grows out of the fear mentality created by the direction of the wave in which the culture has been thus far moving. The downward spiral is pulling harder. Incidents such as Waco, Ruby Ridge, and September 11, are blatant attacks against personal belief systems. The superficial attempts to accept diverse groups of people through hiring quotas have taken a heavy toll on the white Anglo-Saxon male who, coincidentally, has been responsible for a high percentage of the inventions and technological achievements the modern culture displays with pride. Perhaps the growing incidence of prostatic and testicular cancers in this group indicates the results of such an attack on masculinity. Tax burdens increase as the tentacles of government reach further into people's pockets to satisfy the desire to dictate how money will be spent; often it is taken by the government only to be returned with limitations on how it is to be used by the individual. Successful attempts by society to control personal choices through legislation and expensive legal battles are evident in anti-smoking campaigns, car safety, and gun ownership. As these trends take over what individuals may believe and what choices are permitted, individuals will need to develop and rely on courage to recapture their right to freedom of choice or abdicate their inalienable rights of "life, liberty, and the pursuit of happiness." Thus, people would be wise to exercise the great personal power of their own thinking processes, call upon their hearts for discernment of personal truth, clarify their own beliefs, reclaim personal power and responsibility for their actions and decisions, and court the courage of their hearts by overcoming the fear of change.

*Awakening Wisdom from Innocence*

Lately, people are extremely frustrated by the sameness, hidden agendas, and seeming ineptitude of political parties to put forth the will of the people. The birth of this situation was evident in the corporate world some years ago. At that time the purpose of a company was to produce a quality product or service and all members of the company were dedicated to keeping the customer satisfied. An effort to encourage this sense of reliability and concern for the consumer was indirectly promoted by the management's interaction with their staff. Many companies sought to project a family feeling in the work place by recognizing workers' devotion with retirement plans, insurance packages, and job security. This is not as prevalent now because the goal of companies has changed. Although many workers still work toward the satisfaction of the consumer, management's predominant motivation is to satisfy stockholders instead of the customer. This change of purpose by management has led to mass layoffs and downsizing which has led to the end of job security and a reduction in benefits to the worker. The same trend in the government, the redirection of purpose, has resulted in a government dedicated to the economy, not the individuals it was set up to serve. If the people are to reclaim this government and demand accountability to the individual, they will have to courageously oppose unfair practices or dismantle the old, established governing structure, and replace it. That would take a major downpour of unified courage, and the individual members of society would have to project an atmosphere of mutual respect before they could come together as a powerful, courageous group carrying a golden flag of common purpose.

Honor in action equals respect. One truly claims respect by living an honor that shines the truth of love, caring, and validation of individuals spirit coming together in unity. Honor is the unique message of the individual within the oneness, and respect includes the acceptance of the differences. Modern culture desperately needs respect, a resounding individual respect that ripples through the wave of humanity to encompass the people as well as the earth. A blow to personal honor has been wielded by the practices and direction of modern society, and, consequently, by the people as a whole. This heavy-handiness is incrementally increasing and falling upon the heads of younger and younger members of the community as well as the adults. By distorting the personal sense of honor, respect is disappearing and being replaced with crudeness, contempt, and corruption. This is evident in the students at any public school across the country.

This tendency is personified in the actions of a president who admits he lied to millions of Americans, and a society that accepts such actions. The lack of respect for the truth trickles right down through the ranks and replaces the respect of truth with the respect of manipulation of truth for personal gain.

Reclaiming respect for the culture is intricately tied into personal respect and the respect and validation of the diversity and rights of individuals who make up the community membership. This is ultimately possible with strong, confident individuals who contribute their beliefs, talents, and personality. The strength comes from supporting each member in the discovery of who they are and having faith in the blessings of childhood, creative potential, appropriate motivation towards self discovery, unrestricted exploration, and the lack of fear which comes from acceptance and trust in the larger framework of the natural world of spirit.

Many of the aspects of the individual, which once developed and strengthened individually, can be contributed to a loving, supportive community. The reflection of the individual to the culture and the culture to the individual come together in honoring one's self and one another. This honor in action is present in mutual respect, not necessarily agreement of opinion, but a respect and validation of each person's right of freedom of choice. Since modern society often works against one's ability to confidently establish a sense of personal honor based on spiritual truth and unconditional love, the peaceful heart of courage joins the ranks of love, honor, and respect as wisdoms of the heart.

The display of courage during such a major cultural transition will require techniques that vastly differ from the traditional ways of war because the individuals must not engage in battle. That is the old way of thinking in an outdated structure of society. If this new society is going to foster love and independence, tactics which depend on fear for success need to be replaced with methods which encourage voluntary cooperation and entice a personal way of thinking that aligns with the supportive unity's goals. The restructured society has to be flexible enough to allow a place of honor for all, especially the indigenous tribal societies. They understand how to hold a place within the natural world.

If modern culture is to change, and I feel the change is inevitable, there will be incidents of cruelty and death. One might presently look at those killed in Waco as victims of societal change, many of whom were children. The destruction and horror of September 11 also echoes the desire to rid the world of those who believe differently. The question becomes, how does one absorb the horrors and transform the pain into love and acceptance rather than anger and retribution? Herein lies a very crucial challenge for humanity. The manner in which people resolve this issue directly impacts the new cultural path chosen by the group as a whole. If punishment and retaliation cross the fine line of holding a person accountable for their actions and instead makes them the target of unresolved anger, the new societal structure, once again rises up on a foundation of fear and judgment. Although I do not have an easy answer for dealing with cruelty, I believe there are other wisdoms of the heart, forgiveness and compassion that hold the key to freedom nurtured in love and unity.

## Chapter 9

# Forgiveness, Compassion, and Freedom

Just as I desire a society that is more aligned with human potential, this year I desire a garden that reflects the greater potential of the plants that call my garden home. My green gardener's thumb has gone from killing plants to seeing some meager, often fruitless, growth, but this year I am optimistic. I am enjoying the spring and trusting in the natural world. I am going forth trying to live all these lofty thoughts and fine opinions I have shared through my written words. If I am to use them now, the garden is a good place in which to practice creativity, unity, acceptance, and spiritual communication. There is one major obstacle to this year's garden, and it is a very large dead, deeply rooted stump. Within the modern-day society there are also many deeply rooted obstacles. As the removal of the stump causes me physical pain, I am reminded of the pain I can foresee in removing the presently non-productive aspects of modern western society.

*Awakening Wisdom from Innocence*

Last night, as I walked out the back door, I could almost hear that old stump calling to me. I tossed a smile it's way and reflected on the lesson of the stump that so appropriately, although on a much simpler scale, parallels the surmountable problems with directed, conscious, cultural change. The stump that has definitely caused me physical aches, emotional frustration, and fruitless mental exercises, has warmed my spirit and heart with a symbolic lesson in the removal of deeply imbedded, outmoded dying structures. This stump challenges me to think differently, overcome hopelessness based on a limited belief in what is possible, and suggests very strongly that there are lessons for the beliefs one may be subconsciously working on in other seemingly unrelated, everyday living experiences, even the miserable ones. Of course, "miserable" is one of those judgmental words. The potential of such a possibility is phenomenal, and the scope of learning available to those who can move out of the boiling pot and into the pond is awesome.

Thus, I am even feeling gratitude for the presence of the stump because it's presence is asking me to approach the problem by seeking answers in new ways. The illusionary torments at the root of the stump problem fulfill a significant role for me in the direction of my personal growth. Presently, I am inclined to explore a greater understanding of how societal change can come to pass gently. The process of removing the stump expands my skills and calls forth creative potential that I may not have presently recognized within myself. Even if I never remove the stump, it's presence will continue to remind me of the delight I am feeling in realizing that there is so much more to its place in my life. The frustration is such a small part of the total experience when I can expand my thinking to include a greater array of possibilities than just my desire to remove the stump.

Suffering within society has had and apparently continues to serve an important purpose for people. The lessons of Hitler or World War II are as important as those of Christ and astronauts walking on the moon. Each contributes first-hand experience, physical, mental, emotional, and spiritual, to the circle of opposing forces within which modern society functions. Without experiencing both sides, or multiple facets, there would be little meaning in freedom of choice. In order to choose wisely, one needs to intimately know what each choice means. That includes the unpleasant options as well.

*Awakening Wisdom from Innocence*

An important aspect of this process can be seen in the movie Silence of the Lambs. As the movie begins Hannibal Lector's presence makes shivers run up and down the spine of the average person. In Anthony Hopkins' exceptional portrayal, the viewer, of his or her own accord, is sucked deeper into a world of extreme cruelty and dark evil. The viewer experiences terror and disgust. He or she wants to see an end to Hannibal Lector because the horror he exudes from every pore of his being is almost too much to bear. As the movie ends, most viewers express great admiration for Anthony Hopkins and his portrayal of the evil Hannibal Lector. They appreciate the talent that has pulled the terror of an experience in hell from them, but has also delivered them back, unscathed into their routine life. No one hates Anthony Hopkins for temporarily being Hannibal Lector. There is no cry for Anthony Hopkins' execution. Quite the opposite scenario takes place. Anthony Hopkins is celebrated for his believable portrayal and his ability to solicit deep emotional response as Hannibal Lector. The role has expanded his career, and the character of Hannibal Lector has entertained millions.

*Dolores Calley*

There is the possibility that the Genghis Khans, Hitlers, and other evildoers of the world serve a similar function for people as that of the Hannibal Lector—Anthony Hopkins character. Only in one's "real" life, the reality of a spirit taking on the costume of evil has yet to be considered by the masses. I wonder how popular movies would be if when one went to see them, the individuals had to have their minds wiped clean and become part of an ongoing show. And a return to their former life would only become possible when the individual remembered the abundance of the past and charted a path back to the source of life before the movie.

For a long time the species of human beings have been allowed to play freely in an atmosphere of oblivion very much like children enjoying their imaginary worlds while the society revolves around them. Just as children grow into productive awareness of their culture, humankind is approaching that same place of growth on a universal and spiritual level. People are being called upon to recognize the greater universe within which they live and which exists within them and to consciously choose the direction and manner in which they will participate. Opportunities are available to open eyes, hearts, minds, and souls to embrace the changes and consciously direct how this transformation will be brought forth. One can look at the behaviors of children, especially those who have suffered abuse, neglect, fear, and cruelty. One can choose to resort to tantrums, whining, withdrawing, or striking back. Then again, one can choose to model different behaviors, such as kindness, generosity, forgiveness, compassion, and unconditional love. One can honor his or her personal truth and become bold enough to stand up and share that unique authentic piece of the puzzle. As others see this happening, they will be encouraged to follow suit, discovering and blending their individual potential.

John has served as a fine teacher of forgiveness. Even now I doubt he consciously realizes this, yet, he has given me a lifetime opportunity to learn self-forgiveness. And the happiness as a result of this lesson could never have come about without the painful moments. To truly own the outcome because of the struggle; to understand, brings a deeper, longer lasting meaning that integrates with the essence of the being and impacts the belief system.

Since John was my first child, I was lacking confidence in my ability to be a mother. This insecurity stayed somewhere in between John and I because, for a long time, I was unable to resolve it. My personal discomfort in the role of mother was also transferred into an uneasiness in my relationship with my oldest son. In small increments this feeling of dis-ease grew, taking a major leap when I went back to work a year after John's birth.

Feeling uneasy with one's own child can certainly sprinkle guilt into the forming foundation of the relationship. Once Wendel entered the picture and then fell into his world of desperation, demanding a very large portion of my time, energy, and money, John was put on the "back burner". When I stopped to think about John's needs, guilt at my neglect of him handicapped my ability to interact easily and freely with the person into whom he had grown. We locked horns frequently. When I assessed myself in the role as John's mother, I was doing a lousy job. Looking back upon John's childhood, I can see and understand this, but, at the time, I was no more aware of the dynamics than John. The problems between us could easily be rationalized as learning disabilities, negative peer pressure, or any other excuse used for poor communication between parent and child. What I was aware of were the difficulties in communicating with each other, the inability to share differing opinions without taking everything personally, and an overall awkwardness in the relationship. For me, guilt continued to flow, stinging like salt in a wound. The result of my choices made sure of that. John, I must say, never made me feel guilty or badly about his expectations of me as a mother. In fact, John was the opposite, a real supporter of my mothering ability. He was the kind of boy who jumped into my arms, told me that I was the best mom, and often showed appreciation. But I owned the guilt. It was mine. I fed it, wallowed in it, and only I could let it go. Since the problem was mine, demanding or expecting John to change would never truly or completely resolve this issue and bring the relationship to a more satisfying place.

Guilt is far from the only emotion that fosters a growing separation from the loves in one's life. Jealously helps one focus on the potential loss of love. Anger stifles communication. Desperation smothers. Often the world responds and allows a person to reinforce the belief by driving the other person into a new relationship where their loving actions can be seen and appreciated. By carrying disappointment at the expectations that have not been met, one also pushes others out of his or her life. And fear of danger befalling a child often cripples the young one or encourages dangerous behavior.

As my children and I all grew older, I decided to move to California with Michael, thousands of miles away from Florida where Wendel and John were finishing college. I set the two of them up in an apartment, paid for six months rent, and left. Guilty as I felt, I did it; I moved far away. I felt the time had come when my boys needed a mother less than they needed to realize their own strength of character, to rely on their own abilities, and to build their own lives. Maybe I also needed the separation because I was uncomfortable with my older son and just plain exhausted by the demands of the younger one. California was a good choice for me because I needed to be far enough away to keep from interfering, picking up pieces, and watching them struggle out of the cocoon of childhood and into the world of the adult.

I really had no clear idea if I was making the right decision, but once I moved away, I was able to reflect upon my relationship with

*Awakening Wisdom from Innocence*

John and begin to see how my sense of guilt keep John at arm's length. Distance allowed me to see the long-standing situation without the distraction of participating in a continuing, unhealthy, habitual mode of interaction. Until I resolved my guilt and forgave myself for the shortcomings, I would not be able to have the close relationship with John that I deeply desired. I would never know or appreciate the fine man into whom he had grown. Consciously, I set out to do just that, to forgive myself for all the injustices I committed against my first-born and for all the inept moments through which young John had to suffer. Understanding that, although my actions may have been lacking the attention and time I felt they required, my motives were pure; I loved John. It took time but, at last, I was ready to let go of the guilt. During this time of soul-searching I discovered that John knew of little reason for me to ever feel guilty. He loved me. He supported my move to California even though it was an emotionally difficult time for him. My guilt had come from not meeting my own expectations of what a mother should be. Self-forgiveness was hard because I had to look at my perceived lesser aspects of being, my areas of failure. Once the tears and painful remembrances were sifted through and accepted, I began to feel more comfortable and closer to John. Regular spirit chats helped me say all those loving things that a guilty mother has trouble expressing.

There is an interesting full circle aspect to this story. My guilt as John's mother came from my expectations about motherhood and my personal assessment that kept ending up as "failure". Remember my expectations about my desire to complete home improvements by Christmas (Chapter 4), before John and Wendel arrived for the holidays? John decided to leave his job, pack up all his possessions, and come out to stay with Michael and me for a while. John hoped to spend some time with his little brother, figure out his next major move in life, and help me fulfill my home improvement expectations. To update you on the house, the floors were not completed by New Year's Eve. The refrigerator sat in the middle of the floor, but no one, not even me, worried about it.

I understand the value of the process initiated by my home improvement expectations. The drama was not about completion deadlines or the finished product. The expectations brought John and I together working as a partnership, something that my guilt and I denied in our earlier experience. The process of working on the house gave us ample time to talk, reflect on our years together, express gratitude for our presence in each other's life, and, for once, spend easy caring days with one another. For me, John's long visit erased the scar tissue of guilt. Our time together established a new phase in the ongoing life experience we share.

Many parents carry a heavy burden of guilt when it comes to their children. The guilt starts falling like a gentle spring rain when the child is dropped at day care, day after day. The rain increases as the tears of disappointment at missed ball games, concerts, and awards assemblies form little empty pockets of guilt in the relationship's foundation. Teenage years increase the isolation that has formed around the guilt, and the parent hopes that someday, when it is easier, they will have a good relationship with their child. But if the foundation is pockmarked with guilt, fear, disappointment, or any other emotion that fosters separation, the relationship will always fall short because being with your own child will remind you more of failure than success. And neither the success nor the failure will truly be yours. The determination of either is based on judgments and expectations, not on truth and authenticity. Perhaps the accumulated guilt people feel for their lack of proper parenting is reflected in the society's poor, general opinion of children and the low cultural priority that children have become. Ironically, the perception of "poor" parenting is not at all born out of the parents' lack of love. The burden of the misconception also lies with modern, capitalistic society's demands, directives, and view of children. If the society's main priority is amassing wealth, the children take their role from the focus of making money. Thus, the children have value primarily as vehicles for amassing wealth. This view of children can only cause conflict deep within the central core of the parent. At the very essence of each person is a love that wishes to extend to the child as well as the other individuals who make up the society.

The act of forgiveness lifts burdens and breaks up internal dams, allowing the flow of energy and love to return. The result of forgiveness is the release of a greater abundance of creative potential, happiness, love, warm thoughts, and service. This is how forgiveness serves the person who is forgiving. This is why self-forgiveness is important; the act allows one's energy essence and potential to move freely, under consciously directed focus, throughout the body and one's life by removing the blockages that restrict an honest awareness and love for self and others. Continuing to focus energy on maintaining a stance of frustration or anger towards one's self or another causes contraction and kinks within the body and the relationship. Instead of moving in an ever-widening upward spiral of healing and growth, the lack of forgiveness fosters self-chosen stress and disease. The choice is based on the expectations and fears continually encouraged, often demanded, by a society that presently seems to present too many obstacles to individuals comprising it's membership.

Understanding the struggle and complexity that often comes together as a person's life, and allowing for one's humanness, in the same way people give children leeway because they are young and inexperienced, encourages compassion. Compassion for others grows through a camaraderie born out of the difficult lessons one experiences in the emotional, linear, and finite atmosphere of life on earth. By experiencing, accepting, and growing through difficulties and sorrows, individuals can identify with others who have similar hardships, emotional upsets, and obstacles to face. Through discovering one's self, both the strengths and weaknesses, one can recognize that all people have shortcomings as well as talents. If the individual trusts in a divine plan, an all-present God, or the harmony and balance of the natural world, one, by extension, will accept a degree of "rightness" even when a positive affect is not readily visible. And, perhaps, we are all actors in a play taking on different roles to support one another in learning and understanding freedom of choice, love, forgiveness, and other universal truths.

Based on any one of the philosophies presented above, God, divine plan, or natural world, a person will focus on growth from each experience, release the emotional response, and integrate the lesson. The outcome will be revealed as transient, a mere step on an infinite staircase. One may even see the others who are also climbing their way to the top, beyond the clouds and into the cosmos. Once this picture of life on earth is clear and accepted by the individual, compassion is born in the heart. The depth of compassion deepens within an individual, incorporating the insight gained from lessons of hardship, sorrow, lack, and loss, until it finds it's way to spirit. At the level where spirit returns to the source of love, the sea of compassion is deep enough to hold the devil or a Hitler. I cannot honestly say that I am capable of such compassion, but knowing life, the opportunity to swim in a sea of compassion may well present itself. And if challenging myself to love and understand that deeply means that I can participate in a world of beauty, love, and harmony, I say, "Bring the challenge into my life."

If I fail, I still succeed. Through the process, often struggle, to become the spirit of love expressed as compassion, I increase my conscious awareness of how I can bring forth love and compassion in every situation, even the horrible and cruel ones. I reaffirm my commitment to becoming a unique embodiment of love who sustains herself no matter what life brings forth. I become the constant, unalterable truth of the universe. I discover my eternal home. I am free.

*Dolores Calley*

Reawaken Wisdom from Innocence can be purchased from:

>www.1stbooks.com,

>amazon.com

>your local bookstore

For information, contact Dolores Calley at deecalley@hotmail.com

## About the Author

Being a restless spirit Dolores Calley has lived in the North, South, East and West of the country. She has worked as a medical technologist, public school teacher and researcher in Microbiology. Parenting has been the constant in her life. An avid reader and sometimes gardener, Calley has a love of humanity, especially the young, a keen eye for observation, especially those things that are out of sync with the cultural picture, and a penchant for independent thinking. Presently, Dolores lives in North Carolina with her youngest son. AWAKENING WISDOM FROM INNOCENCE is her first book.

Printed in the United States
6345